MADAGASCAR
Simple Guide

A Complete Guide to Hidden Wonders, Local Traditions, Breathtaking Landscapes, and Everything You Need to Know for a Seamless and Unforgettable Trip

Wendell Leitz

COPYRIGHT

© 2025 Wendell Leitz. All rights reserved.

No part of this book may be reproduced, stored in a retrieval system, or transmitted in any form or by any means, electronic, mechanical, photocopying, recording, or otherwise, without prior written permission from the publisher, except for the use of brief quotations in a review or scholarly work.

DISCLAIMER

The information provided in this book is intended as a general travel guide. While every effort has been made to ensure the accuracy of the content, the author and publisher are not responsible for any errors, omissions, or inaccuracies that may arise. Travelers are encouraged to do additional research, consult local authorities, and exercise discretion when making travel decisions. The author and publisher disclaim any liability for any injuries, losses, or damages sustained while following the advice or recommendations in this book.

TABLE OF CONTENT

INTRODUCTION...10
CHAPTER 1..**13**
  WELCOME TO MADAGASCAR....................... 13
    Quick Facts: Location, Size, and Identity....14
    A Brief Cultural Snapshot........................... 17
CHAPTER 2... **19**
  TRAVEL ESSENTIALS YOU SHOULD KNOW 19
    Entry Requirements and Travel Documents.. 19
    Currency, Exchange Tips, and Mobile Money 20
    Languages Spoken and Key Local Phrases. 22
    Safety and Health Tips for a Stress-Free Trip. 24
    What to Pack..27
    What to Leave Behind................................ 29
CHAPTER 3...**32**
  BEST TIME TO VISIT MADAGASCAR............32
    Understanding the Seasons: Dry and. Rainy.. 32
    Best Time for Wildlife Watching and Outdoor Adventures......................................35
    Peak Travel Months vs. Quieter Periods.....38
      Peak Travel Months (July to August)....38
      Quieter Periods (April to June & September to November).......................39

Rainy Season (November to March)......40
Local Festivals and Events Worth Planning Around..41
Festival of the Baobab (July to August) 42
Alahamady Be (January).......................42
Donia Festival (May).............................43
Madajazzcar Festival (October/November)................................43
Foire Internationale de Madagascar (October)...44

CHAPTER 4..45
GETTING TO AND AROUND MADAGASCAR... 45
International Entry Points and Main Airports...45
Domestic Flights and Inter-City Travel Options..48
Buses, Taxis, and Local Transport (What's Safe and What's Not)...................................52
Buses and Taxi-Brousse.........................52
Taxis..53
Motorcycles and Rickshaws....................54
Safety Considerations............................55
Renting Vehicles and Hiring Local Guides. 56
Renting Vehicles.....................................56
Hiring Local Guides................................58

CHAPTER 5...60
WHERE TO STAY IN MADAGASCAR..............60

Types of Accommodation: From Budget to Luxury.......... 60
   Staying in Cities and Staying Near Nature 64
Tips for Booking and What to Look For......67
   Start Early, Especially During Peak Seasons...................................68
   Read Reviews and Do Your Research... 68
   Confirm Availability and Ask About Facilities.................................69
   Consider the Location and Accessibility.... 70
   Check for Family-Friendly or Group Options................................70
Responsible Stays and Eco-Lodges............ 71
   Choose Eco-Friendly Properties........... 71
   Support Local Communities.................72
   Wildlife Conservation........................... 73
   Carbon Footprint Offset Programs........73
   Respect the Environment..................... 74

CHAPTER 6..75
WHAT TO EAT AND DRINK IN MADAGASCAR................................. 75
Popular Traditional Dishes and Street Food.. 75
   Ravitoto (Pork with Cassava Leaves).... 76
   Romazava (Beef Stew).......................... 76
   Zebu Meat...77

Malagasy Street Food: Koba and Mofo Gasy.................77
Saka Saka (Cassava Leaves with Peanut Sauce)..................78

Regional Flavors and Must-Try Meals........78
Coastal Delights: Seafood and Fish.......78
Antananarivo (Capital City) Specialties 79
Highland Region: Rice and Meat-Based Dishes.................. 80
Southern Madagascar: Spicy and Tasty 80
The East Coast: Sweet and Savory Dishes. 80

Drinks to Try in Madagascar......................81
Rum (Rhum Arrangé)...........................81
Fresh Fruit Juices................................82
Malagasy Tea.......................................82
Beer and Local Wines..........................82

Beverages and Local Treats.......................83
Traditional Beverages..........................83
Local Sweets and Snacks...................... 85

Where to Eat: Markets, Local Spots, and Restaurants.................................. 86
Local Markets.......................................87
Local Restaurants and Dining Spots.....88
Eco-Friendly and Responsible Dining.. 90

Food Safety Tips and What to Avoid...........91
Food Safety Tips...................................91
What to Avoid...................................... 93

7

CHAPTER 7..96
   TOP DESTINATIONS AND WHAT TO EXPECT. 96
      Antananarivo – The Capital City................ 96
      Nosy Be – The Island Escape......................101
         Why It's Popular Among Travelers...... 101
         Reaching Nosy Be................................. 102
         Beach Resorts and Affordable Lodging..... 103
         Snorkeling, Diving, and Island Tours..104
         Foods and Nightlife..............................105
      Avenue of the Baobabs – Nature's Monument... 106
         The Magic of the Baobab Trees............106
         How to Get There................................. 107
         Sunrise/Sunset Viewing Tips................108
         Nearby Villages and Cultural Encounters. 109
      Isalo National Park – Canyon and Stone Wonderland... 111
         Scenic Hikes and Wildlife...................... 111
         Where to Stay Near the Park................ 112
         Guided Tours and Trail Advice.............113
         What to Bring and What to Know........ 115
      Andasibe-Mantadia – The Lemur Capital. 116
      Tsingy de Bemaraha – The Stone Forest...119

CHAPTER 8... **123**
   HIDDEN GEMS AND OFF-THE-PATH
   ADVENTURES... 123
CHAPTER 9... **128**
   THINGS TO DO IN MADAGASCAR.............. 128
CHAPTER 10..**133**
   THINGS YOU SHOULDN'T DO..................... 133
CHAPTER 11... **139**
   SAMPLE ITINERARIES................................. 139
CHAPTER 12..**146**
   RESPONSIBLE TRAVEL IN MADAGASCAR 146
   CONCLUSION...156

INTRODUCTION

Madagascar is a land of wonder, where nature's diversity comes alive in every corner of the island. From towering baobabs to lush rainforests and unique wildlife found nowhere else on Earth, Madagascar is a destination unlike any other. It's not just a place to visit; it's a place to experience. Whether you're drawn to its mesmerizing landscapes, its fascinating creatures, or its vibrant culture, there's something magical waiting for every traveler. But with so much to explore, how do you make the most of your trip?

This guide is designed to simplify your journey and ensure you don't miss out on the island's most incredible experiences. While there are many resources out there, this book stands out because it combines practical travel tips with a deep dive into the beauty and culture of Madagascar. It goes beyond the basic tourist information, offering insights that will help you navigate the country with ease, explore hidden gems, and understand the rich traditions of this unique island. This guide doesn't just tell you where to go—it helps you immerse yourself fully in the spirit of Madagascar, providing a thorough yet easy-to-follow roadmap for your adventure.

This book is for anyone with a sense of adventure, whether you're a seasoned traveler or embarking on your first international trip. If you want to explore Madagascar's wild landscapes, taste its delicious cuisine, and discover its rich history, this guide is for you. It's perfect for travelers who want to experience the authentic side of the island, off the beaten path, without the confusion of overwhelming travel resources.

To get the most out of this guide, read it before you go and use it as a companion during your travels. You'll find useful information on everything from transportation and accommodation to the best places to eat, things to do, and tips on how to interact with the local people respectfully. Each section is designed to be easy to follow, providing you with the essentials you need to explore Madagascar in the most fulfilling way possible.

CHAPTER 1

WELCOME TO MADAGASCAR

Welcome to Madagascar, a place where nature and adventure come together in perfect harmony. Imagine an island brimming with unique landscapes, from its sprawling beaches to its dense rainforests and towering mountains. It's a land where the unexpected happens at every turn—where wildlife, plants, and traditions come together to create a truly magical experience. Whether you're strolling through the Avenue of the Baobabs, hiking through dense jungles, or exploring untouched beaches, Madagascar promises an experience like no other.

What makes Madagascar so special is that it is an island of contrasts. It is the world's fourth largest island, and it remains relatively untouched compared to many other popular travel destinations. It is home to a range of ecosystems that have developed independently over millions of years, leading to a stunning array of species that can be found nowhere else on Earth. From the playful lemurs to the striking chameleons, the island is a haven for wildlife lovers and photographers alike. But it's not just nature that stands out—it's the people and their deep connection to the land and culture that makes Madagascar an unforgettable experience.

Quick Facts: Location, Size, and Identity

Madagascar is located in the Indian Ocean, just off the southeastern coast of Africa. It's separated from mainland Africa by the Mozambique Channel, about 400 kilometers (250 miles) away. This island is the fourth-largest in the world, covering an area of around 587,000 square kilometers (227,000 square miles), roughly the size of France.

Madagascar is known for its rich biodiversity, with around 90% of its wildlife being endemic, meaning it is found nowhere else in the world. Its diverse ecosystems include tropical rainforests, dry deserts, and highland plateaus, all of which create a captivating mix of nature and adventure. The country's culture is equally diverse, with influences from African, Arab, Asian, and European ancestry, making it a melting pot of traditions, languages, and cuisine.

Madagascar's identity is deeply rooted in its people. With over 22 ethnic groups, the Malagasy people have a strong sense of community and family. Their way of life is intertwined with the land, and their respect for nature is reflected in the island's many sacred sites, traditional practices, and vibrant festivals.

Madagascar is a living testament to the wonders of nature. The island's ecosystems are not just varied; they are unique in the truest sense of the word. With its isolation from other landmasses for millions of years, Madagascar has evolved into a natural paradise that harbors life forms found nowhere else on Earth. This diverse range of ecosystems is what makes the island so special.

From the lush rainforests that cover its eastern slopes to the dry, spiny forests in the south, Madagascar's landscapes are a photographer's dream and an explorer's haven. The island's biodiversity is world-renowned, with an astonishing 90% of its plant and animal species being endemic. The famous lemurs, ranging from the tiny mouse lemur to the more robust indri, are perhaps the most iconic inhabitants. But the island's wildlife doesn't stop there. You'll find striking chameleons, colorful geckos, and hundreds of bird species, including the rare Madagascar fish eagle. Madagascar's flora is just as fascinating, with plants like the baobab tree, whose ancient, twisted trunks seem to defy gravity.

One of the most exciting aspects of Madagascar's ecosystems is how easily they can be explored. Whether you're trekking through the rainforests, hiking the highlands, or walking across the otherworldly spiny forests, every corner of the island offers a chance to encounter a world unlike any other. The island is also home to many national parks and reserves, like Ranomafana and Andasibe-Mantadia, which are must-see destinations for anyone interested in the island's rich biodiversity.

A Brief Cultural Snapshot

While Madagascar's wildlife and landscapes are undoubtedly captivating, its culture adds another layer of intrigue to the island. The Malagasy people, with their deep-rooted traditions and customs, offer a warm and welcoming atmosphere to visitors. The culture of Madagascar is an amalgamation of African, Asian, Arab, and European influences, reflecting the island's long history of migration and trade.

The Malagasy language is the primary language spoken, although French is also widely used, especially in urban areas. Music, dance, and storytelling are central to Malagasy life, with regional differences giving rise to unique styles and traditions. The island's vibrant festivals, like the famadihana (the turning of the bones) and the annual hiragasy performances, provide visitors with an opportunity to experience Madagascar's rich cultural heritage firsthand.

Cuisine is another reflection of Madagascar's diverse cultural influences. The food is as unique as the island itself, with staples like rice and zebu (a type of cattle) being integral to meals. Expect to find a mix of African, Asian, and European flavors, all fused together in Malagasy dishes. Fresh seafood, tropical fruits, and the distinctive Malagasy spices will make your culinary adventure as memorable as your journey through the island's landscapes.

CHAPTER 2

TRAVEL ESSENTIALS YOU SHOULD KNOW

Before setting off on your adventure to Madagascar, it's important to ensure that you're well-prepared for the journey. Understanding the entry requirements, having the right travel documents, and being aware of how to handle currency and money while traveling are essential for a smooth and hassle-free experience.

Entry Requirements and Travel Documents

To enter Madagascar, most travelers will need a valid passport with at least six months of validity beyond their intended stay. A visa is also required for entry, but the process is straightforward for many nationalities. You can obtain a tourist visa upon arrival at the airport, which is usually valid for up to 30 days. However, it's always a good idea to check the specific visa requirements based on your nationality before you travel, as rules can sometimes change.

Additionally, if you plan to stay longer than 30 days or engage in activities like volunteering or business, you may need to apply for a different type of visa before you arrive. To make sure everything is in order, it's wise to carry a copy of your return ticket and proof of sufficient funds to cover your stay. It's always best to keep your documents in a safe place during your travels, such as a money belt or a hotel safe, to avoid any issues while exploring the island.

Currency, Exchange Tips, and Mobile Money

The local currency in Madagascar is the Malagasy Ariary (MGA), and it is essential to have cash on hand, especially in rural areas where credit card facilities may be limited. While larger cities and popular tourist destinations will have ATMs and exchange services, smaller towns and remote regions often do not, so it's important to plan accordingly.

Currency exchange can be done at major banks or at authorized exchange offices. However, keep in mind that exchange rates can vary, so it's always a good idea to compare rates before exchanging large amounts of money. It's also recommended to exchange your money in larger cities, where you'll find better rates and more reliable services. Some hotels and tour operators may accept US dollars or euros, but this is not always guaranteed, so it's best to carry local currency for everyday purchases.

Mobile money services, like Orange Money and Airtel Money, are also widely used in Madagascar. These services allow you to send and receive money, pay for services, and even withdraw cash from agents or ATMs. If you're planning to stay for an extended period, it might be useful to set up a mobile money account upon arrival, as it offers a convenient and safe way to manage your funds. You can easily load your mobile money account at local agents, and using it for transactions is often quicker and more secure than carrying large sums of cash.

When traveling to Madagascar, it's important to familiarize yourself with the languages spoken and understand some basic local phrases that will help you navigate the island. Communication can be a bit challenging outside the major cities, as not everyone speaks English, but knowing a few key phrases can make your journey much easier and more enjoyable.

Languages Spoken and Key Local Phrases

Madagascar's official languages are Malagasy and French, with Malagasy being the most widely spoken across the country. French is commonly used in government, business, and tourism-related activities, especially in urban areas. While English is not as prevalent, many hotels, restaurants, and tour operators may have staff who can speak basic English.

Here are a few useful Malagasy phrases that could come in handy:

- **Hello:** Manao ahoana (ma-na-o ah-ho-na)

- **How are you?** Inona ny vaovao? (ee-noh-nah nee vah-vah-oo?)

- **Thank you:** Misaotra (mee-sao-tra)

- **Yes:** Eny (eh-nee)

- **No:** Tsia (tsee-ah)

- **Please:** Azafady (ah-zah-fah-dee)

- **Goodbye:** Veloma (veh-loo-mah)

If you're traveling to more rural areas, it might also be helpful to learn a few words or phrases in French, especially if you're going to be interacting with people in urban areas or local businesses. A little effort to speak the local language can go a long way in making connections and showing respect for the culture.

Safety and Health Tips for a Stress-Free Trip

Ensuring a safe and healthy trip to Madagascar is essential, and with a bit of preparation, you can enjoy your adventure without any major concerns. While the island is generally safe for tourists, it's always wise to stay cautious and take some basic health and safety measures.

Safety Tips: Madagascar is a relatively safe destination, but like any place, it's important to stay aware of your surroundings, particularly in crowded areas or unfamiliar parts of towns. Petty theft, such as pickpocketing, can occur in busy markets or public transport, so keep your belongings secure at all times. It's advisable to avoid walking alone at night, especially in unfamiliar areas, and always use reputable taxi services or arrange transportation through your hotel.

Health Tips: When it comes to health, it's crucial to take some basic precautions. First and foremost, make sure you're up to date on routine vaccinations and consider travel vaccinations for diseases like typhoid, hepatitis A, and B. Malaria is present in some parts of Madagascar, so consult with your healthcare provider about malaria prevention before you travel. It's also a good idea to carry a first-aid kit with essentials like bandages, pain relievers, and insect repellent.

Drinking tap water in Madagascar is not recommended for tourists, so be sure to only drink bottled water. Avoid ice in drinks and peel fruits and vegetables before eating them to minimize the risk of foodborne illnesses. Be cautious when consuming street food, and stick to stalls that look clean and busy, as this is often an indication of fresh and well-prepared food.

For a smooth trip, also make sure to have travel insurance that covers health emergencies and any potential issues during your stay. Being prepared for unforeseen circumstances can give you peace of mind and ensure that you can enjoy your time in Madagascar without stress.

Packing for a trip to Madagascar can be both exciting and a bit overwhelming, given the island's diverse landscapes, varying climates, and adventurous activities you might want to enjoy. Knowing what to pack (and what to leave behind) is key to ensuring a comfortable and hassle-free journey. Here's a guide to help you prepare the right essentials for your adventure.

What to Pack

Clothing for All Seasons:

Madagascar's weather can vary significantly depending on the region and time of year, so packing layers is essential. If you're visiting the rainforest or the cooler highlands, bring long sleeves and pants to protect yourself from mosquitoes and other insects. On the other hand, the coastal areas are generally warm and tropical, so pack light, breathable clothing such as cotton t-shirts, shorts, and a swimsuit for beach destinations.

If you're planning on hiking or exploring the rugged landscapes, sturdy, comfortable shoes are a must. Hiking boots or good walking shoes will serve you well on Madagascar's sometimes rough and uneven terrain. Don't forget a hat and sunglasses for sun protection, especially if you plan to spend a lot of time outdoors.

Insect Protection:

Due to Madagascar's tropical climate, it's important to pack items to protect yourself from insects. Malaria is present in certain parts of the island, so don't forget to bring insect repellent with DEET and anti-malaria medication if recommended by your doctor. A lightweight, long-sleeved shirt and long pants are useful for evening walks when mosquitoes are more active.

Medical Essentials and First-Aid Kit:

A first-aid kit should be part of your packing list, especially for hikes or if you plan to visit more remote areas. Include items like band-aids, antiseptic cream, pain relievers, and any personal medications you may need. If you wear glasses or contact lenses, bring extra pairs, as they can be difficult to find in rural areas.

Power and Electronics:

Electricity supply can be inconsistent in some parts of Madagascar, so it's a good idea to bring a power bank to keep your devices charged during long days of exploration. If you plan on using your phone for navigation, photography, or communication, make sure it's unlocked and able to work with a local SIM card. Adapters are also important, as Madagascar uses the European plug type (two round pins).

Travel Essentials:
Don't forget the basics like your passport, travel insurance details, and a printed copy of your flight itinerary. It's also wise to have some cash in the local currency (Malagasy Ariary) on hand for small purchases, as many places, especially in rural areas, may not accept credit cards. A reusable water bottle is also a good idea, especially since you'll want to stay hydrated while exploring Madagascar's diverse landscapes.

What to Leave Behind

Heavy Luggage:
While it might be tempting to pack everything "just in case," try to keep your luggage as light as possible. Overpacking can be a hassle when you're

traveling from one place to another, especially if you plan on visiting remote areas or taking public transport. Stick to the essentials and pack light clothing that can easily be washed and dried. Avoid bringing anything that can be easily purchased on the island.

Valuable Jewelry and Expensive Electronics: Madagascar is generally safe for tourists, but it's always wise to leave expensive jewelry and high-end electronics at home. Carrying valuable items can make you a target for petty theft, especially in crowded or unfamiliar areas. If you do bring electronics like cameras or laptops, ensure they are well-secured and stored in your hotel safe when not in use.

Non-Essential Items:
Don't overload your bags with non-essential items like heavy books, unnecessary accessories, or extra shoes. Space and weight are limited, and you'll want to make sure you have room for souvenirs or items you pick up along the way. Think practically and

aim for versatility in your packing to make your travel experience more enjoyable.

CHAPTER 3

BEST TIME TO VISIT MADAGASCAR

When planning your trip to Madagascar, understanding the island's climate and seasons will help you determine the best time to visit. Madagascar's diverse landscapes and ecosystems mean that weather conditions can vary widely depending on the region, making it essential to consider the best seasons for both your comfort and the activities you want to enjoy.

Understanding the Seasons: Dry and Rainy

Madagascar has two main seasons: the dry season and the rainy season. The dry season typically runs from April to October, while the rainy season lasts from November to March. Each season offers unique advantages and challenges, depending on what you're hoping to experience during your trip.

- **Dry Season (April to October):**

    The dry season is considered the best time to visit Madagascar, especially for outdoor activities like hiking, wildlife watching, and exploring the island's unique landscapes. Temperatures are more moderate, ranging from 18°C to 25°C (64°F to 77°F), which makes it comfortable for exploring. The dry weather also means less chance of rain, which can make transportation and travel between destinations easier. Many national parks are more accessible during this time, and wildlife sightings are often better as animals gather around the remaining water sources.

- **Rainy Season (November to March):**

    The rainy season brings heavier rainfall, especially from December to February, and it can make travel in certain parts of Madagascar more challenging due to muddy roads and flooded trails. However, the rain also transforms the island into a lush, vibrant paradise. If you're looking for fewer crowds and don't mind the wet conditions, the rainy season can offer a more tranquil experience. The temperature during this time tends to be warmer, ranging from 25°C to 35°C (77°F to 95°F), and it's a great time for seeing the island's botanical beauty in full bloom.

In general, if your primary focus is exploring the natural beauty of the island without too many weather-related disruptions, the dry season is the best time to visit. However, if you want to avoid crowds and experience Madagascar's rich green landscapes, the rainy season offers a different, yet equally enchanting, atmosphere.

Best Time for Wildlife Watching and Outdoor Adventures

Madagascar is renowned for its unique wildlife, and timing your visit according to the best seasons for wildlife watching can greatly enhance your experience. The dry season is undoubtedly the best time for spotting animals, as many species tend to be more visible around the waterholes, and the vegetation is less dense, making it easier to spot wildlife. If you're visiting Madagascar specifically for wildlife encounters, here's a closer look at the best times to visit different regions for specific experiences:

- **Lemur Watching:**
  Lemurs are perhaps Madagascar's most iconic animals, and you'll find them in national parks across the island. The dry season (April to October) is ideal for lemur watching, as they are more active during the cooler mornings and evenings. If you want to see specific species, such as the famous

ring-tailed lemurs or the indri, make sure to plan your visit to the appropriate parks during these months.

- **Bird Watching:**

  Madagascar is home to over 100 species of birds that are found nowhere else on Earth, making it a paradise for bird watchers. The best time for bird watching is during the dry season, when the birds are more easily spotted in the open and are often more active. The rainy season can still offer good bird watching, but the dense foliage may make spotting birds more challenging.

- **Whale Watching:**

  If you're planning to visit the coastal areas for whale watching, the best time to go is from June to September when humpback whales migrate to Madagascar's waters to breed and give birth. You'll have the opportunity to witness these magnificent creatures in action, especially near the islands of Nosy Be and Sainte-Marie.

- **Hiking and Exploring National Parks:** Madagascar's varied terrain offers incredible hiking opportunities, and the dry season is the best time for outdoor adventures. Whether you're trekking through the Avenue of the Baobabs, hiking in the Isalo National Park, or exploring the otherworldly landscapes of Tsingy de Bemaraha, the dry season provides more stable weather and better trail conditions. While some parks are still accessible during the rainy season, be prepared for muddy and slippery trails, which can make hikes more challenging.

In short, if wildlife watching, outdoor exploration, and photography are your primary interests, the dry season is your best bet for optimal conditions. However, the rainy season, with its lush scenery and fewer crowds, can also offer a unique and

37

peaceful experience, especially for those who appreciate Madagascar's rich flora and fauna in a more tranquil setting.

Peak Travel Months vs. Quieter Periods

When planning your trip to Madagascar, it's essential to consider the flow of tourists and how that can impact your experience. Like many popular destinations, Madagascar has peak travel periods and quieter times, each offering its own set of advantages. Understanding these periods will help you decide when to visit, based on your preference for crowds, activities, and overall experience.

Peak Travel Months (July to August)

The peak travel months in Madagascar coincide with the dry season, particularly in July and August. This is the winter period in the Southern Hemisphere, making it the most comfortable time to visit. During these months, the weather is cooler and drier, and the conditions are ideal for outdoor activities like hiking, wildlife watching, and exploring national parks. As a result, you can expect an influx of international tourists, especially families and vacationers.

While it's the best time to explore Madagascar, the downside is that popular tourist destinations can get crowded, and accommodation prices may rise. It's wise to book your accommodations and tours well in advance if you're traveling during this period.

Quieter Periods (April to June & September to November)

For those looking to avoid the crowds, the shoulder seasons of April to June and September to November are ideal. The weather during these months is still pleasant, with moderate temperatures and less rain. While the dry season may be coming to a close or just beginning, the crowds are generally smaller, meaning you can enjoy the stunning landscapes and wildlife without the hustle and bustle.

In these quieter months, you'll also have a more authentic experience of Madagascar, where you can connect with locals and experience the culture more intimately. However, some parks and sites may be a little less accessible during the shoulder months, especially toward the tail end of the rainy season in April and May. Still, the quieter, less commercialized environment makes it an excellent time for those seeking solitude and tranquility.

Rainy Season (November to March)

The rainy season is considered the off-peak period for Madagascar, which means fewer tourists and lower prices. While this can be a great time to experience a more serene Madagascar, it's important to note that the weather can be unpredictable. Roads may be muddy, and certain remote regions might be difficult to access, making it less ideal for extensive travel or outdoor activities.

The tropical rains tend to fall in short bursts, so there's still a chance for clear skies in between the showers.

If you don't mind the wet conditions and prefer a quieter trip with fewer tourists, the rainy season offers the best opportunity to visit for a peaceful and relaxed experience.

Local Festivals and Events Worth Planning Around

Madagascar's rich cultural heritage is reflected in its many festivals and events throughout the year. From traditional ceremonies to vibrant celebrations, attending a local festival can provide deeper insight into the island's culture and traditions. However, timing your trip around these events can also offer an opportunity to experience Madagascar in a truly special way.

Festival of the Baobab (July to August)

The Festival of the Baobab is a celebration of the island's iconic baobab trees, which are native to Madagascar. Held in the Menabe region, this festival includes cultural performances, music, dances, and traditional ceremonies honoring the trees, which are considered sacred by the local communities. If you're visiting Madagascar in July or August, this festival offers a unique chance to witness Madagascar's cultural diversity and the reverence locals hold for the island's natural wonders.

Alahamady Be (January)

Alahamady Be is Madagascar's traditional New Year celebration, typically taking place in January, and is one of the most important cultural events on the island. It's celebrated with feasts, music, dances, and family gatherings. Different regions of Madagascar observe this festival with their own specific customs and rituals, and if you're in the country during this time, you'll experience the vibrant spirit of Malagasy culture. This event is ideal for those looking to immerse themselves in local traditions and celebrations.

Donia Festival (May)

Held annually in Nosy Be, the Donia Festival is one of Madagascar's largest music festivals. It features live performances from artists across the island, showcasing the diverse sounds of Malagasy music. With reggae, traditional Malagasy rhythms, and international acts, this festival is perfect for music lovers looking to experience the island's dynamic cultural scene. If you plan to visit Madagascar in May, attending the Donia Festival is a fantastic way to enjoy music, dance, and the tropical island vibe.

Madajazzcar Festival (October/November)

For jazz enthusiasts, the Madajazzcar Festival in Antananarivo is a must-visit. Held annually in the capital city, this event brings together local and international jazz musicians for a series of concerts and performances. It's one of the most important cultural festivals for jazz lovers in the region and a unique opportunity to experience Madagascar's modern musical side. If you're in Madagascar during October or November, don't miss the chance to enjoy some of the best live jazz performances the island has to offer.

Foire Internationale de Madagascar (October)

This international trade fair, held in Antananarivo, is one of Madagascar's largest events, attracting businesses, tourists, and locals alike. The fair showcases local products, crafts, food, and tourism-related services. If you're interested in learning more about Madagascar's industries, products, and culture, attending the Foire Internationale de Madagascar can give you an insider's view into the island's economic landscape.

CHAPTER 4

GETTING TO AND AROUND MADAGASCAR

Traveling to and around Madagascar can be an adventure in itself, with various ways to reach the island and explore its many regions. Here's what you need to know to navigate your way to and through this beautiful country.

International Entry Points and Main Airports

Madagascar is well connected to international destinations, primarily through its capital city, Antananarivo, and a few other major airports. Most international travelers will arrive at one of these key entry points.

Ivato International Airport (Antananarivo)

The main gateway to Madagascar is Ivato International Airport, located in the capital city, Antananarivo. It handles the majority of international flights coming to the island. Airlines from various regions, including Europe, Africa, Asia, and the Indian Ocean islands, operate flights to and from Ivato. If you're flying from Europe, you'll likely have a stopover in countries like France or Mauritius before heading to Madagascar. From the airport, you can easily access the city, where you'll find accommodations and transportation options.

Nosy Be Fascene International Airport (Nosy Be)

If you're heading to the popular tourist destination of Nosy Be, you'll land at Fascene International Airport. This airport is the second most significant international entry point to Madagascar, serving travelers who are visiting the island's beaches, resorts, and diving spots. While not as busy as

Antananarivo, Fascene Airport still has good connections with destinations like Réunion and Mauritius.

Antsiranana (Diego Suarez) Airport (Antsiranana)

Another option for those traveling to northern Madagascar is Antsiranana (also known as Diego Suarez) Airport. This airport serves the city of Antsiranana and provides domestic flights, but a few international flights, mainly from neighboring countries, also land here. If you're interested in exploring Madagascar's north, this is an excellent entry point.

Other Airports

Madagascar has a few other smaller airports located in major cities and tourist regions. These include airports in Toliara (for access to the southwest), Mahajanga (for the northwest), and Fort Dauphin (for the southeastern coast). These airports mainly handle domestic flights and are less frequently used by international travelers, but they are useful if you're already within the country.

Domestic Flights and Inter-City Travel Options

Madagascar is a large island with a variety of terrains, making domestic travel an important aspect of any visit. Here are the primary ways to get around the island once you arrive.

Domestic Flights

One of the easiest and fastest ways to travel between regions in Madagascar is by taking a domestic flight. Air Madagascar (also known as Tsaradia) operates a range of domestic flights connecting Antananarivo with other major cities and tourist destinations such as Nosy Be, Mahajanga, Toliara, and Fort Dauphin. These flights are convenient but can be subject to delays, so it's best to plan accordingly and check the schedules ahead of time. Booking in advance is recommended, especially during peak tourist seasons, as flights can fill up quickly.

Taxi-Brousse (Shared Minibus)

For those looking for an affordable and adventurous way to travel, taxi-brousse is the most popular form of inter-city transport in Madagascar. These shared minibuses travel between towns and cities and are a great way to see the country from the road. Although not the most comfortable mode of transport, they are inexpensive and provide a real Malagasy experience. Taxi-brousses are generally available from the main bus stations in Antananarivo and other large cities, and while they may not be the fastest, they do offer a great opportunity to meet locals.

Private Taxis and Car Rentals

Private taxis and car rentals are available throughout Madagascar, but driving can be challenging due to the sometimes poor condition of the roads. If you're planning on renting a car, it's best to have an experienced driver who knows the terrain. If you prefer not to drive, private taxis can be hired for longer trips, but make sure to agree on the price beforehand, as there are no meters. Renting a vehicle with a driver can be a good option if you're traveling to more remote areas where public transport may not be as reliable.

Train Travel

Madagascar has a limited but charming rail network that connects some of the country's main cities, such as Antananarivo, Fianarantsoa, and Manakara. The train rides are relatively slow but offer a scenic and unique way to travel. The train system is not as reliable as other transport options, and services may be interrupted by weather or maintenance issues, so it's important to check the schedules in advance if you plan on using this option.

Boats and Ferries

For travelers heading to the coastal regions or islands, boats and ferries are a popular option. Regular ferry services operate between the mainland and various smaller islands, including Nosy Be, Île Sainte-Marie, and the island of Nosy Komba. While these services are reliable, they may not always be comfortable, especially during the rainy season when the seas can be rough. Be sure to check schedules in advance and prepare for the varying sea conditions.

Local Transportation (Rickshaws, Tuk-Tuks, and Motorbikes)

Within cities, you'll find a variety of local transportation options such as rickshaws, tuk-tuks, and motorbikes. These are ideal for short trips around town, and the prices are typically very affordable. It's a great way to get around the busy streets of Antananarivo or other urban areas. Always negotiate the fare beforehand or ensure the driver uses a meter if available.

Buses, Taxis, and Local Transport (What's Safe and What's Not)

Navigating Madagascar's cities and towns can be an exciting experience, but it's essential to be aware of local transportation options, safety concerns, and how to make the most of them.

Buses and Taxi-Brousse

The most common form of transportation for long-distance travel in Madagascar is the taxi-brousse, or shared minibus. These buses run between cities and towns, offering an affordable and reliable way to get around. However, it's important to know that the experience can vary widely in terms of comfort and reliability. The buses are often crowded and may not follow a strict schedule. They tend to stop frequently to pick up and drop off passengers, and the ride can be bumpy, especially on unpaved roads. While taxi-brousses are a budget-friendly option, they may not be the best choice for those seeking comfort or who are traveling on a tight schedule.

As for city buses, these are available in some of Madagascar's larger cities but are less common in rural areas. The schedules and routes can be confusing for visitors, so it's often easier to rely on other forms of transport when moving around urban centers.

Taxis

In Madagascar's larger cities like Antananarivo, taxis are a popular mode of transport. While they are relatively easy to find, taxis in Madagascar generally do not use meters, so it's important to agree on a price before starting the journey. Be sure to discuss the fare beforehand to avoid misunderstandings. While most taxi drivers are friendly, it's always best to ask locals for recommendations on reputable drivers. It's also wise to avoid taking a taxi alone late at night or in poorly lit areas for safety reasons.

In general, taxis are a convenient way to get around, especially for short distances within the city. However, since taxi prices can vary, make sure to have a rough idea of what the fare should be for your journey to avoid being overcharged.

Motorcycles and Rickshaws

Motorcycles and rickshaws are commonly used for short-distance travel, especially in smaller towns or in the more rural areas. In the capital, you'll find tuk-tuks, which are a quick and cheap option for getting around town. Rickshaws are another form of local transport that may be available in certain areas, but these can be less reliable.

When using motorcycles or tuk-tuks, it's important to wear a helmet for safety. While some drivers may provide helmets, it's always good to bring your own to ensure your safety. It's also recommended to agree on the fare before you embark on the ride.

Safety Considerations

Although public transport in Madagascar is generally safe, there are a few things to keep in mind to ensure your safety and comfort:

- **Avoid traveling at night**. Public transport, especially taxi-brousses, can be risky after dark. It's best to plan your travels during daylight hours.

- **Watch your belongings**. Like in many places around the world, pickpocketing can be an issue in crowded public transport areas. Keep your valuables secure and be cautious with your personal items.

- **Choose reputable companies**. When using taxis or renting vehicles, try to go with established companies or trusted recommendations from locals. For example, most hotels can help you book a reputable taxi or guide.

Renting Vehicles and Hiring Local Guides

For those who prefer more independence or want to explore more remote areas of Madagascar, renting a vehicle or hiring a local guide can enhance your experience. Here's what you should know about these options.

Renting Vehicles

Renting a car in Madagascar is an excellent option for travelers wanting to explore the island at their own pace. While driving can be a fun way to see the countryside, it's important to note that road conditions can be challenging. Many roads, especially in rural areas, are poorly maintained and may not be paved. In addition, driving styles in Madagascar can be unpredictable, so it's important to drive with caution.

Car Rental Tips:

- **Rental companies**. There are several car rental companies in major cities like Antananarivo, but many of them require international drivers' permits. Make sure to check with the rental agency about the specific requirements.

- **4x4 vehicles**. If you're planning to visit remote or rugged areas, a 4x4 vehicle is recommended as it will allow you to tackle off-road conditions with greater ease.

- **Costs**. Rental rates vary, but they are generally affordable compared to Western countries. However, you should be prepared for additional fees such as insurance, fuel, and optional services like a driver or GPS.

- **Local Driving Laws**. In Madagascar, driving is on the right-hand side of the road.

Always adhere to local driving laws and be aware of the road conditions, which can change drastically depending on the area you're in.

If you're not comfortable with driving in Madagascar, you can often rent a car with a local driver. Many companies offer this option for an extra fee. Having a local driver is not only a good way to avoid potential driving hazards, but it also provides you with insider knowledge of the country and its culture.

Hiring Local Guides

Hiring a local guide can be a great way to make the most of your trip to Madagascar. Local guides are knowledgeable about the island's history, culture, and wildlife, and they can help you navigate less-developed areas where English is not widely spoken. Guides can also provide insights into local traditions and customs, making your experience much richer.

Why Hire a Guide:

- **Expert knowledge**. Local guides can show you hidden gems, such as little-known parks, waterfalls, or villages, that you might not discover on your own.

- **Cultural connections**. Having a guide can also help you interact with local communities in a respectful way, which enhances the cultural experience.

- **Navigation**. In more remote areas, having a guide is not only helpful but often necessary, especially for off-the-beaten-path destinations. They are familiar with the geography and can ensure you get to your destination safely.

When hiring a guide, make sure they are certified by the relevant tourism authorities in Madagascar. Many reputable guides can be booked through hotels, tour agencies, or national parks.

CHAPTER 5

WHERE TO STAY IN MADAGASCAR

When visiting Madagascar, your choice of accommodation will depend on your budget, preferences, and the areas you plan to explore. Whether you're looking for a simple guesthouse or a luxurious resort, the island offers a wide range of options to suit every traveler's needs. Here's a breakdown of the types of accommodations you can expect, as well as insights into staying in cities versus staying near nature.

Types of Accommodation: From Budget to Luxury

Madagascar offers a wide variety of accommodations, catering to all budgets. From simple guesthouses to all-inclusive resorts, you'll find something that fits your needs. Here's a closer look at the different types:

BUDGET ACCOMMODATION

Guesthouses and Hostels: If you're traveling on a tight budget, guesthouses and hostels are excellent options. These accommodations are often run by local families or small businesses and provide a comfortable, yet affordable, stay. In cities like Antananarivo and smaller towns across the island, you'll find basic amenities, such as a bed, shared bathrooms, and sometimes a small kitchen. They are a great choice for backpackers or those looking to spend their money on experiences rather than luxury accommodations.

Campsites: For those who prefer being closer to nature, camping can be a great option. There are designated campsites in national parks and nature reserves, where you can experience Madagascar's wildlife up close. While facilities might be basic, you'll be immersed in the natural beauty of the island.

MID-RANGE ACCOMMODATION

Boutique Hotels and Lodges: If you're looking for something in the middle, boutique hotels and lodges offer more comfort and amenities, without the steep price tag. These establishments often feature private rooms, en-suite bathrooms, Wi-Fi, and sometimes even swimming pools and restaurant services. They are typically located in popular tourist areas, close to beaches, nature reserves, or city centers. The atmosphere in these places tends to be more personal and cozy, often with a focus on Malagasy culture and hospitality.

Eco-Lodges: Eco-lodges are becoming increasingly popular for travelers who are keen on sustainability. Located in or near national parks, eco-lodges are built to minimize environmental impact while offering comfort and authenticity. Many of these lodges have rustic designs and integrate local materials, blending well with their natural surroundings.

LUXURY ACCOMMODATION

Resorts and High-End Hotels: For those who prefer a more luxurious stay, Madagascar is home to a number of high-end resorts and international hotel chains. These accommodations offer superior amenities such as spas, fine dining restaurants, and stunning views of the ocean or rainforests. The luxury resorts are typically found in coastal areas or remote natural retreats, offering both relaxation and adventure with activities like snorkeling, diving, or hiking right at your doorstep.

Private Villas: Another option for those seeking exclusivity is renting a private villa. These are especially popular for families or groups traveling together, providing both privacy and luxury. Many villas come with personal chefs, staff, and exclusive access to private beaches or remote areas, making for a truly indulgent stay.

Staying in Cities and Staying Near Nature

Madagascar offers two distinct experiences when it comes to where you choose to stay: the bustling cities and the tranquil natural landscapes. Both options have their advantages, depending on your preferences.

- **Staying in Cities**:

    - **Urban Experience**: Staying in Madagascar's cities, such as Antananarivo, Nosy Be, or Toamasina, offers a more urban experience. These cities provide access to a variety of restaurants, shops, and cultural attractions, including museums, markets, and local events. You'll also find better infrastructure, such as medical services, transportation options, and a wider selection of accommodations.

- **Convenience**: If you prefer a more organized and comfortable environment, staying in the city can be the best option. Cities have reliable electricity, Wi-Fi, and an array of amenities that can make your stay more convenient and enjoyable.

- **Nightlife and Dining**: In urban areas, you can experience Madagascar's vibrant food scene and nightlife, from casual street food stalls to fine dining restaurants. You'll also find bars, clubs, and live music venues to explore once the sun goes down.

- **Staying Near Nature**:

    - **Close to Wildlife and Outdoor Adventures**: For nature lovers, staying near Madagascar's natural wonders is a must. Whether you're in a lodge in the rainforests of Andasibe, an eco-lodge near the famous Avenue of the Baobabs, or a beachfront bungalow in Nosy Be, staying near nature puts you in the heart of Madagascar's incredible biodiversity. You'll wake up to the sounds of chirping birds, the rustling of leaves, and the calls of lemurs.

- **Peace and Tranquility**: Nature-based accommodations tend to be more serene and peaceful, offering a retreat from the hustle and bustle of daily life. Many of these properties are remote and offer minimal distractions, making them ideal for relaxation, yoga, meditation, or simply enjoying the outdoors.

- **Access to Adventure**: If you want to explore Madagascar's famous national parks, such as Ranomafana, Isalo, or Masoala, staying near these parks will give you easy access to trekking, wildlife watching, and scenic hikes. You can also book guided tours to explore unique landscapes like the Tsingy de Bemaraha or the beautiful beaches of Nosy Be.

Tips for Booking and What to Look For

When planning your accommodation in Madagascar, booking ahead can make your trip smoother and more enjoyable, especially if you're traveling during the peak tourist season. Here are some practical tips to help you book the best places to stay, along with things to look for to ensure a hassle-free experience:

Start Early, Especially During Peak Seasons

Madagascar's peak tourist season typically runs from July to October, which means accommodation tends to fill up quickly during this time. If you're planning to visit during these months, it's advisable to book your stay well in advance. For off-peak seasons, you may find that prices are lower, and availability is better, but some accommodations in remote areas may close or have limited services during the rainy season.

Read Reviews and Do Your Research

Always check online reviews and ratings before booking any accommodation. Websites like TripAdvisor, Booking.com, or Airbnb can provide valuable insights into the quality and service of a place. Look for recent reviews to gauge the level of customer satisfaction and to see how the property holds up over time.

Be sure to pay attention to reviews regarding cleanliness, staff friendliness, and the accuracy of descriptions. This will give you a clear idea of what to expect when you arrive.

Confirm Availability and Ask About Facilities

It's always a good idea to contact the accommodation directly to confirm availability, especially if you're traveling to more remote locations. Ask about the facilities, like Wi-Fi access, electricity, water supply, and whether there are any additional fees for services such as guided tours, meals, or transportation.

Also, check if they offer anything unique, like cultural experiences, nature hikes, or local excursions, which could enhance your trip.

Consider the Location and Accessibility

Depending on your itinerary, it's essential to think about the location of your accommodation. If you plan on exploring national parks or other nature spots, staying nearby will reduce travel time and costs. If you prefer city life, look for accommodations that are close to the main attractions, shops, restaurants, and transportation hubs.

Keep in mind that Madagascar's infrastructure can be limited, so confirm how accessible the accommodation is, especially if you are staying in remote areas. Some places may require a longer journey or additional transport arrangements.

Check for Family-Friendly or Group Options

If you're traveling with children or in a group, look for places that cater to families or large groups. Some accommodations provide family rooms, kid-friendly amenities, or organized group activities like guided tours. Make sure the environment is safe and suitable for all ages.

Responsible Stays and Eco-Lodges

In recent years, Madagascar has seen a rise in eco-tourism, with more travelers seeking responsible stays that minimize environmental impact while supporting local communities. If sustainability is important to you, choosing eco-lodges or accommodations with a focus on conservation and responsible tourism can be a rewarding choice. Here's what to look for:

Choose Eco-Friendly Properties

- **Sustainable Practices**: Look for accommodations that follow eco-friendly practices, such as reducing energy consumption, minimizing water usage, and reducing waste. Many eco-lodges in Madagascar use solar panels, offer recycling programs, and practice water conservation.

- **Use of Local Materials**: Eco-lodges often use local and sustainable materials for construction, which helps minimize their environmental footprint. They may also integrate traditional Malagasy architecture, which blends seamlessly with the natural environment.

Support Local Communities

- **Local Hiring and Fair Wages**: Many eco-lodges and responsible stays hire local staff, helping to provide employment opportunities and support the local economy. This also ensures that your stay contributes to the well-being of the community.

- **Cultural Immersion**: Responsible stays may offer cultural experiences such as local cooking classes, crafts workshops, or village tours, allowing you to connect with the Malagasy people while supporting their traditions.

Wildlife Conservation

- **Involvement in Conservation Efforts**: Some eco-lodges and nature-based accommodations collaborate with wildlife conservation projects, such as protecting endangered species or preserving Madagascar's unique ecosystems. By staying at these places, you can directly contribute to these efforts through your stay and potentially even participate in wildlife-related activities or programs.

Carbon Footprint Offset Programs

- Many eco-lodges offer ways to offset your carbon footprint through tree planting initiatives or donations to local environmental causes. Ask about their commitment to sustainability and whether they have programs to help mitigate the environmental impact of tourism.

Respect the Environment

- As a guest, you also have a role in promoting responsible tourism. Respect the natural environment by following guidelines set by the accommodation, such as avoiding littering, staying on designated trails, and not disturbing wildlife. Supporting businesses that prioritize sustainability helps ensure that Madagascar's unique ecosystems can be enjoyed by future generations.

CHAPTER 6

WHAT TO EAT AND DRINK IN MADAGASCAR

Madagascar is a land of unique flavors and culinary traditions that reflect its diverse culture and geography. Whether you're dining at a local street food stall or enjoying a meal in a high-end restaurant, there's something for every palate. Here's an exploration of the must-try dishes and beverages you should savor during your visit.

Popular Traditional Dishes and Street Food

Madagascar's food is heavily influenced by its mix of African, Asian, and French heritage. The traditional Malagasy diet is simple yet packed with flavor, and it's largely centered around rice, vegetables, and a variety of meats and seafood. Street food in Madagascar is also a great way to taste authentic local flavors while experiencing the bustling atmosphere of the cities and markets.

Ravitoto (Pork with Cassava Leaves)

One of the most beloved Malagasy dishes, ravitoto is made from finely shredded cassava leaves cooked with pork. It's a rich, hearty dish typically served with rice, making it a filling and comforting meal. It's often accompanied by a side of spicy sambal (chili sauce) to add a kick to the flavor.

Romazava (Beef Stew)

Romazava is a flavorful beef stew made with a mix of greens, including Malagasy mustard leaves, and cooked with a blend of spices. This dish is considered the national dish of Madagascar and is often enjoyed with rice. The combination of tender meat and earthy vegetables makes it a satisfying and wholesome meal.

Zebu Meat

Zebu, a type of cattle native to Madagascar, is often cooked in various ways—grilled, roasted, or stewed. It's a popular protein source and is typically prepared in dishes like *brochettes* (grilled skewers) or served in stews and soups. Zebu meat has a distinct, rich flavor and is a must-try for meat lovers.

Malagasy Street Food: Koba and Mofo Gasy

Koba: A traditional Malagasy dessert made from ground rice, peanuts, and brown sugar wrapped in banana leaves. It's a sweet, nutty treat often sold in street markets as a snack.

Mofo Gasy: A popular breakfast street food, mofo gasy is a type of Malagasy pancake made from rice flour and served hot, often accompanied by tea or coffee. It's soft and slightly sweet, perfect for a light start to your day.

Saka Saka (Cassava Leaves with Peanut Sauce)

Saka saka is another beloved Malagasy dish made from cassava leaves, which are boiled and simmered in a rich peanut sauce. The creamy and flavorful sauce adds a distinct taste to the dish, which is often served with rice and sometimes accompanied by meat or fish.

Regional Flavors and Must-Try Meals

Madagascar's cuisine is diverse, with regional variations that offer a unique taste of the island's geography and culture. From the coastal seafood dishes to the mountain-based recipes, each region brings its own specialty to the table.

Coastal Delights: Seafood and Fish

Madagascar's extensive coastline offers an abundance of fresh seafood. Dishes featuring fish, shrimp, lobster, and crab are commonly served in coastal areas. One popular dish is *achard de légumes*, which is a pickled vegetable side dish that pairs perfectly with fresh fish or grilled seafood.

Vary Amin'anana (Rice with Greens and Fish): A staple in coastal areas, this dish consists of rice topped with a mixture of herbs, greens, and often, fish. It's a fresh and healthy meal, typically enjoyed with a light broth.

Antananarivo (Capital City) Specialties

In Madagascar's capital, Antananarivo, you'll find an interesting blend of French and Malagasy cuisine. For example, mofo baolina (fried dough balls) and bary madio (simple rice dish with vegetables) are street snacks you can find in the bustling streets.

French-influenced meals, like *croissants* or *baguettes*, are often served at cafes in the city, reflecting the colonial history.

Highland Region: Rice and Meat-Based Dishes

In the highlands, rice is a staple food, and meals are often served with meat, especially zebu, or with beans. *Vary amin'anana* (rice with greens) and *lasary* (a side of vegetables or salads) are frequently eaten here. The region also enjoys hearty meat stews and roasted meats.

Southern Madagascar: Spicy and Tasty

The southern region of Madagascar is known for its spicy food and more arid climate. Dishes are often centered around dried meats, lentils, and legumes. One dish unique to the south is *Kary*, a spicy stew made with meats and legumes that's perfect for the hot, dry climate.

The East Coast: Sweet and Savory Dishes

The lush and tropical east coast of Madagascar is known for its sweet and savory dishes that incorporate exotic fruits such as coconut, bananas, and pineapples. You might also find flavorful curries here, made with locally grown spices and herbs. *Vary sosoa* (rice with seafood) is a common dish in the region.

Drinks to Try in Madagascar

Madagascar's beverage scene is as diverse as its cuisine, offering both refreshing drinks and unique local concoctions.

Rum (Rhum Arrangé)

Madagascar is known for its rum production, and you'll find locally produced rhum arrangé, which is a spiced rum infused with fruits, herbs, and other flavors. It's an essential drink to try while visiting the island. The rum is often served in small shots or mixed into cocktails.

Fresh Fruit Juices

Madagascar is home to a wide variety of tropical fruits, so fresh fruit juices are popular across the island. You'll find juices made from pineapple, mango, guava, and tamarind, served cold and refreshing, perfect for a hot day.

Malagasy Tea

Madagascar produces high-quality tea, particularly in the highland areas. Tea is often served with sugar and milk, or sometimes with spices. It's a comforting drink, particularly in the cooler regions of the island.

Beer and Local Wines

Local Malagasy beer is widely available, with brands like *THB* (Three Horses Beer) being popular among both locals and tourists. You might also find some local wines, typically light and fruity, produced in the island's growing wine regions.

Beverages and Local Treats

Madagascar is not only known for its exotic cuisine but also for its refreshing beverages and sweet local treats. Whether you're in the mood for a refreshing drink to cool you down or craving a sweet snack to enjoy with your afternoon tea, Madagascar offers a delightful range of options.

Traditional Beverages

Rhum Arrangé

This is perhaps the most iconic drink in Madagascar. Rhum Arrangé is a local rum that's often infused with fruits, herbs, and spices. The concoctions vary from one region to another, and it's usually served as a digestif after meals. The most common varieties include rum with vanilla, passionfruit, or even coconut.

Tropical Fruit Juices

Madagascar's tropical climate is home to an abundance of fruits, and fresh fruit juices are a popular beverage choice. You'll find juices made from pineapple, mango, guava, tamarind, and more. The fruit juices are usually made fresh and served chilled, making them perfect for cooling off on a hot day.

Bière Madagascar (Madagascar Beer)

For beer enthusiasts, Madagascar offers local brews such as *THB* (Three Horses Beer), which is widely available throughout the island. The beer is light, crisp, and refreshing—perfect for pairing with a meal or enjoying during your visit to the local markets.

Malagasy Tea

The cool highlands of Madagascar are home to some of the best tea production in the world. Malagasy tea is known for its smooth taste, and it's often served with milk or sugar. It's a popular beverage to sip on during the cooler evenings.

Koba (Local Sweet Treat)

Koba is a beloved traditional dessert made of rice flour, peanuts, and sugar, wrapped in banana leaves. This sweet, nutty treat is commonly sold at street stalls and markets. It's perfect for those with a sweet tooth and a great snack to enjoy while exploring the island.

Mofo Gasy (Malagasy Pancakes)

Mofo Gasy is another delightful treat that locals enjoy for breakfast or as an afternoon snack. These soft, slightly sweet rice flour pancakes are typically served hot and are delicious when dipped into tea or coffee. They're widely sold in markets, making them an easy and tasty snack to grab while you're on the go.

Local Sweets and Snacks

Boudin (Black Pudding)

A popular street food in Madagascar, boudin is a type of black pudding made with pork and rice. It's often served with a spicy sauce and is a popular savory snack to eat on the go.

Ravitoto with Rice

Though traditionally a main meal, this dish made from cassava leaves and pork is sometimes enjoyed as a snack in smaller portions. The bitterness of the cassava leaves combined with the rich flavors of the pork and spices creates a unique and satisfying snack.

Saka Saka

Saka Saka is another savory treat made from cassava leaves cooked in a peanut sauce. While it is often a part of a larger meal, it's also served as a snack at many local food stalls.

Where to Eat: Markets, Local Spots, and Restaurants

Madagascar offers a variety of dining experiences, from bustling street food markets to fine dining restaurants offering local and international cuisine.

Whether you're looking for an authentic Malagasy experience or simply want to try some fusion dishes, Madagascar has something for everyone.

Local Markets

Analakely Market (Antananarivo)

If you're in Madagascar's capital, Antananarivo, don't miss the vibrant Analakely Market. Here, you'll find a wide range of fresh produce, spices, and street food. It's a great place to sample local Malagasy snacks like *mofo gasy* (pancakes), fresh fruits, and traditional dishes such as *koba* and *saka saka*. The market is also perfect for picking up unique souvenirs to take home.

Zoma Market (Antsirabe)

In the city of Antsirabe, Zoma Market offers a similar experience, but with more regional specialties. In addition to fresh produce and spices, you'll find local artisan products and handicrafts. You'll also have the chance to try *kary* (a spicy stew) and sample local fruits and vegetables from the highlands.

Nosy Be Markets (Nosy Be Island)
Nosy Be, known for its tropical climate, also boasts several bustling markets where you can enjoy fresh seafood and local delicacies. You'll find local fish dishes, crab, and other seafood, as well as delicious fruit-based juices. The markets here are great places to meet local vendors and learn about their cuisine.

Local Restaurants and Dining Spots

La Varangue (Antananarivo)
La Varangue is one of the top fine-dining restaurants in the capital city. It combines French-influenced cuisine with local Malagasy ingredients, offering a unique fusion experience. The restaurant is known for its warm ambiance and attentive service, making it a perfect place to enjoy a special dinner while in Antananarivo.

Chez Arol (Antananarivo)

For an authentic Malagasy meal in Antananarivo, Chez Arol is a popular choice. Here, you can enjoy traditional Malagasy dishes like *romazava* (beef stew), *ravitoto* (cassava leaves with pork), and *saka saka*. The prices are affordable, and the atmosphere is casual, making it a great spot to enjoy the flavors of Madagascar.

Le Jardin d'Antananarivo (Antananarivo)

For those who appreciate a tranquil setting while dining, Le Jardin d'Antananarivo offers a peaceful garden atmosphere with a mix of Malagasy and European dishes. The restaurant is known for its fresh produce and friendly service, and it's a great option for a relaxing lunch or dinner.

L'Hotel Colbert (Antananarivo)

Another excellent choice in the capital, L'Hotel Colbert features a top-tier restaurant that serves both international and Malagasy cuisine. The restaurant is located within a luxury hotel, providing a more refined dining experience. It's a great place to try the island's best dishes, such as *zebu steak* and *achard de légumes* (pickled vegetables), while enjoying stunning views of the city.

Eco-Friendly and Responsible Dining

Eco-Lodges and Local Dining Experiences

For those looking for a more sustainable dining experience, many eco-lodges and local community-run restaurants across Madagascar prioritize fresh, locally sourced ingredients and environmentally friendly practices. Staying in eco-lodges often means enjoying meals prepared with produce grown in organic gardens, and some places even offer cooking classes so you can learn how to make traditional Malagasy dishes yourself.

Responsible Dining Practices

When eating in Madagascar, it's important to choose restaurants and eateries that support local communities and focus on sustainable practices. Look for eateries that source their ingredients locally, especially when it comes to seafood, to ensure that you're supporting responsible fishing practices.

Food Safety Tips and What to Avoid

When traveling to Madagascar, food safety is an important aspect to consider. The island offers a delightful array of local dishes, but like any other destination, it's essential to be mindful of what you eat and drink to avoid any unpleasant experiences. Here are some food safety tips and things to avoid during your trip:

Food Safety Tips

Drink Bottled Water

In Madagascar, it's advised to drink bottled water instead of tap water. While the local water may be safe in some areas, there's always a risk of contamination, especially in rural parts. Make sure the bottle is sealed before purchasing, and avoid using ice cubes unless you're sure the water used is filtered.

Eat Freshly Cooked Food

Opt for food that is freshly cooked to order. Street food is delicious and an integral part of the Malagasy experience, but make sure it's served hot. Eating freshly prepared meals ensures that bacteria, which may have multiplied on food left exposed for too long, are minimized.

Avoid Raw Foods

While you may be tempted by raw foods like sushi or uncooked salads, it's better to avoid them in Madagascar. The local hygiene standards can vary, and raw vegetables and fruits may have been washed in untreated water, increasing the risk of illness. Always choose cooked meals where possible.

Check Food Quality

When eating at local markets or smaller eateries, ensure the food looks fresh and is being handled properly. Watch how food is stored and prepared, and if you notice any suspicious practices or unclean conditions, it's best to skip that food stall.

Be Cautious with Dairy

Dairy products in Madagascar, especially if not stored correctly, can be risky. Unrefrigerated dairy products like milk and cheese should be avoided, as they may not be pasteurized or may have been sitting out in hot conditions for too long.

Clean Your Hands Regularly

Handwashing is crucial when traveling in Madagascar. Carry hand sanitizer with you and use it before eating, especially if you've been in public places or touching surfaces that may have bacteria. Some areas may lack proper facilities for handwashing, so it's best to stay prepared.

What to Avoid

Unpeeled Fruits and Vegetables

While fresh fruits and vegetables are abundant in Madagascar, it's best to avoid eating them unpeeled unless you can wash them with clean water. Opt for fruits that you can peel yourself, such as bananas, oranges, and mangoes. For vegetables, choose ones that have been thoroughly cooked.

Ice Cubes from Untrusted Sources

In many places, ice is made from tap water, which may not be safe. Unless you are certain the ice is made from purified water, it's better to avoid iced drinks, particularly at street vendors or remote locations where water quality is less regulated.

Street Food that's Been Sitting Out

Street food is a part of the culture in Madagascar, but be cautious about food that has been sitting out for a while, especially meats and fish. Bacteria grow quickly in hot, humid conditions, so it's best to eat food that has just been prepared.

Non-Sealed Packaged Foods

Be cautious of packaged foods that aren't sealed properly. Some local products, especially those sold at markets or roadside stalls, may not have been stored or sealed correctly. Always inspect packaging for any signs of damage or tampering before purchasing packaged snacks or bottled drinks.

Excessive Spicy Food

Malagasy food can be quite spicy, but if you're not accustomed to heat, it's best to avoid dishes with excessive spice, particularly those served at informal or roadside eateries. While the spiciness can be part of the local experience, it may lead to stomach upset for sensitive eaters.

CHAPTER 7

TOP DESTINATIONS AND WHAT TO EXPECT

Antananarivo – The Capital City

Antananarivo, often abbreviated as Tana, is the bustling capital and largest city of Madagascar. Located in the central highlands, this city is a vibrant mix of colonial architecture, traditional Malagasy culture, and modern developments. While it may not boast the tropical allure of coastal regions, Antananarivo is the heart of the island's political, economic, and cultural life. As the gateway to Madagascar, it's a fascinating place to start your journey.

How to Get There and Around

Antananarivo is accessible via Ivato International Airport, which welcomes both international and domestic flights. Many major airlines offer direct flights from destinations such as Paris, Johannesburg, and Nairobi, making it relatively easy to get to Madagascar from most parts of the world. Once in the city, getting around is fairly straightforward. You can opt for taxis or use local transportation options like "taxi-brousse" (shared minivans) for more affordable travel. Be prepared for traffic in the city, especially during rush hours, as Antananarivo is known for its congestion.

Where to Stay

In Antananarivo, there are accommodations to suit every budget, from luxury hotels to guesthouses. If you're looking for comfort, consider staying in the city center, where you'll find higher-end hotels like Hotel Colbert or Radisson Blu. For those on a budget, there are a variety of affordable hostels and guesthouses, such as Maison Lovasoa or Hotel La Ribaudière. For a unique experience, you could even book a stay in a traditional Malagasy guesthouse for an authentic cultural experience.

Places to Visit

Antananarivo offers several places of interest for those wanting to explore the city. The Royal Palace, or Rova of Antananarivo, offers stunning views over the city and a glimpse into the island's royal history. The Ambohimanga Hill, a UNESCO World Heritage Site, is another cultural landmark, where you can learn about the historic significance of the Malagasy monarchy. The Tsimbazaza Zoo and Botanical Gardens are perfect for nature lovers and families, providing an opportunity to see some of Madagascar's unique wildlife.

For a deeper dive into the local culture, visit the Analakely Market for a taste of everyday life, or explore the numerous art galleries and museums that showcase the island's rich artistic heritage, such as the Musée d'Art et d'Archéologie.

Local Dishes to Try

While in Antananarivo, you must indulge in the Malagasy cuisine. Try dishes like *romazava* (a meat and greens stew), *zebu* (local beef) served with rice, or *ravitoto* (cassava leaves with pork). Street food is also a big part of the city's food scene, with vendors offering snacks like *mokary* (rice cakes) and *koba* (a sweet treat made from rice flour, peanuts, and sugar). Don't forget to try *masikita* (grilled meat skewers), commonly served with fresh salads.

Best Experiences and Practical Tips

Antananarivo offers more than just sightseeing; it's also an excellent place to immerse yourself in local culture. For a unique experience, take a walking tour of the city's historical neighborhoods, where you can admire the colonial-era architecture and vibrant markets. Explore the colorful streets of the Upper Town, where the views over the city are breathtaking. If you're a nature enthusiast, take a short hike to the nearby hills or visit one of the many gardens scattered around the city.

Practical Tips:

- **Weather:** The city experiences a mild climate, with cool temperatures in the highlands. Pack layers, as temperatures can vary throughout the day.

- **Safety:** Antananarivo is generally safe for tourists, but as in any large city, it's important to stay vigilant, especially in crowded areas and after dark. Keep your belongings secure and avoid walking alone in poorly lit areas.

- **Local Etiquette:** Malagasy people are known for their hospitality, but it's important to respect local customs. When greeting people, a firm handshake is common. Dress modestly, particularly when visiting religious or cultural sites.

Antananarivo is not just a transit hub; it's a vibrant city full of history, culture, and culinary delights. Whether you're exploring its historic landmarks, sampling its local cuisine, or simply strolling through its lively streets, the capital offers a great introduction to Madagascar's diverse and welcoming spirit.

Nosy Be – The Island Escape

Why It's Popular Among Travelers

Nosy Be, often referred to as the "perfumed island," is one of Madagascar's most famous tourist destinations. Located off the northwest coast, it's known for its stunning beaches, crystal-clear waters, and laid-back island atmosphere. Nosy Be has earned its reputation as a tropical paradise, attracting travelers seeking relaxation, adventure, and a dose of natural beauty. Whether you're looking to unwind on pristine beaches or explore vibrant marine life, Nosy Be offers a blend of both worlds. It's also a popular destination for those wanting to experience Madagascar's unique biodiversity, as the island is home to rare flora and fauna.

Reaching Nosy Be

To get to Nosy Be, the most convenient way is by air. Nosy Be Fascene Airport offers regular flights from Antananarivo, the capital, as well as from other parts of Madagascar. Flights are relatively short, usually taking about an hour, making Nosy Be easily accessible for both domestic and international travelers. You can also reach Nosy Be by boat, especially if you're coming from nearby islands or coastal areas like the mainland port of Ankify, where you can catch a ferry to the island.

For those coming from abroad, you can fly into Antananarivo and then catch a connecting flight to Nosy Be. International airlines such as Air Madagascar and Air Austral operate flights to the island, making it an easy addition to your Madagascar itinerary.

Beach Resorts and Affordable Lodging

Nosy Be is home to a range of accommodations that cater to different budgets. From luxury beach resorts to affordable guesthouses, there's something for everyone. For those looking for high-end comfort, consider staying at one of the island's luxury resorts like the Andilana Beach Resort or the Nosy Be Hotel & Spa, which offer all-inclusive services, private beaches, and world-class amenities.

If you're traveling on a budget, there are plenty of more affordable options. Guesthouses and small hotels offer comfortable rooms at reasonable prices, with many located near the beach for easy access to the island's attractions. For a more immersive experience, you can also book eco-lodges, which are a popular choice among those seeking to experience Nosy Be's natural beauty while minimizing their environmental impact.

Snorkeling, Diving, and Island Tours

Nosy Be is a paradise for water lovers, offering some of the best snorkeling and diving opportunities in Madagascar. The island is surrounded by coral reefs, and the clear waters are home to an incredible variety of marine life, including tropical fish, sea turtles, and even whale sharks. You can book snorkeling or diving tours with local operators, many of whom provide all the necessary equipment and guide you to the best spots around the island.

For those interested in a more relaxed experience, island tours are a fantastic way to explore Nosy Be's surrounding islands. You can visit Nosy Komba, home to the famous black lemurs, or take a boat trip to Nosy Tanikely, a marine reserve that offers pristine snorkeling conditions. Another popular tour is to the smaller island of Nosy Saba, known for its untouched nature and peaceful surroundings.

Foods and Nightlife

Nosy Be offers a great variety of dining options, from beachfront restaurants serving fresh seafood to local eateries offering traditional Malagasy dishes. You can sample dishes like *zebu* steak, *romazava*, and *koba* (a delicious snack made from peanuts and rice flour). Seafood lovers will particularly enjoy the fresh catches of the day, including lobster, fish, and prawns, all prepared with local spices and served with rice or cassava.

When the sun sets, Nosy Be comes alive with vibrant nightlife. The island has a laid-back but lively bar scene, with many beach resorts offering evening entertainment. You can enjoy cocktails and Malagasy rum while watching the sunset, and then head to one of the island's nightclubs or live music venues for a more energetic experience. The nightlife here is not overwhelming but provides a great opportunity to socialize with fellow travelers and locals alike.

Nosy Be is a place where adventure and relaxation coexist, offering everything from thrilling water sports to peaceful evenings by the beach. Whether you're exploring its marine life, enjoying its food, or simply soaking in the island's tranquil vibe, Nosy Be is sure to leave you with unforgettable memories of your Madagascar adventure.

Avenue of the Baobabs – Nature's Monument

The Magic of the Baobab Trees

The Avenue of the Baobabs is one of Madagascar's most iconic and awe-inspiring natural landmarks. Stretching along a dirt road near Morondava on the west coast, this remarkable site is home to a cluster of towering baobab trees that appear like something out of a dream. These unique trees, known for their massive trunks and odd, otherworldly shapes, stand like silent sentinels against the sky. The baobab trees, which can grow to over 30 meters in height and live for over a thousand years, are often called the "upside-down trees" because their branches resemble roots reaching for the sky.

The Avenue of the Baobabs is not just a place of natural beauty, but it's also considered sacred by the locals. The trees are a part of Madagascar's rich cultural and spiritual heritage, and many locals view them as guardians of the land. Visiting this avenue allows you to witness the power and mystique of nature, while also connecting with Madagascar's deep-rooted traditions.

How to Get There

The Avenue of the Baobabs is located about 45 minutes' drive from the coastal town of Morondava, which is the nearest major city. Morondava is accessible by road and domestic flights from Antananarivo, the capital of Madagascar. Once you arrive in Morondava, you can rent a 4x4 vehicle to reach the Avenue, as the road can be quite bumpy and rugged.

Traveling to the Avenue of the Baobabs can be part of an unforgettable road trip through Madagascar's western regions. There are also organized tours from Morondava that offer a more hassle-free experience, with guides who can help explain the significance of the area and provide deeper insights into the culture and natural wonders of the region.

Sunrise/Sunset Viewing Tips

The Avenue of the Baobabs is most famous for its breathtaking sunrise and sunset views. The way the light hits the trees at these times of day creates a surreal and magical atmosphere, with the baobabs casting long shadows on the dirt road and the sky painted in shades of orange, pink, and purple.

For the best experience, aim to arrive early in the morning or late in the afternoon. Sunrise typically occurs around 5:30 AM to 6:00 AM, while sunset is between 5:30 PM and 6:00 PM, depending on the season. Early mornings tend to be quieter, allowing you to enjoy the tranquility of the place before the crowds arrive. In the evenings, the golden hour offers incredible photographic opportunities, so be sure to have your camera ready to capture the stunning scenes.

To make the most of your visit, consider bringing a tripod if you're interested in capturing long-exposure shots of the baobabs against the changing sky. The low light at sunrise and sunset creates perfect conditions for dramatic and striking photos.

Nearby Villages and Cultural Encounters

The Avenue of the Baobabs is located near several traditional Malagasy villages, where you can get a glimpse into the everyday lives of the local people. The village of Belo-sur-Tsiribihina is the closest settlement to the Avenue, and visiting it offers an opportunity to engage with local communities. Many locals here practice farming, fishing, and craft-making, and they are often happy to share their stories and culture with visitors.

You can also explore the local markets, where you might find handmade goods such as baskets, jewelry, and woven textiles. These items are often made using traditional techniques passed down through generations, and purchasing them can support the local economy.

If you're interested in a deeper cultural encounter, consider visiting a local family or joining a community-run tour. These experiences offer a chance to learn more about the region's history, customs, and way of life, making your visit to the Avenue of the Baobabs even more meaningful.

The Avenue of the Baobabs isn't just about its trees—it's about the entire experience, from the stunning natural beauty to the rich cultural connections that make it a truly unforgettable destination in Madagascar. Whether you're looking for an epic photo opportunity, a peaceful escape, or a cultural adventure, this place has something to offer every traveler.

Isalo National Park – Canyon and Stone Wonderland

Scenic Hikes and Wildlife

Isalo National Park is a true gem of Madagascar, known for its otherworldly landscapes that combine rugged canyons, dramatic rock formations, and lush valleys. Often referred to as Madagascar's "Grand Canyon," Isalo offers some of the most stunning and diverse scenery on the island. The park's unique geology, shaped by millions of years of erosion, creates natural wonders such as sandstone formations, deep gorges, and cascading waterfalls. It's a place where adventure and natural beauty seamlessly blend.

The park is also home to a variety of wildlife, including several species of lemurs, chameleons, and endemic birds. Visitors often encounter the ring-tailed lemur, which is one of Madagascar's most famous inhabitants. As you hike through the park, you'll hear the calls of various birds and maybe spot the elusive sifaka lemur, which is known for its elegant leaps between trees. The diverse ecosystems, from dry scrubland to tropical forests, provide ample opportunities for wildlife watching, making Isalo a must-visit for nature lovers and photographers alike.

Where to Stay Near the Park

While Isalo National Park is known for its breathtaking outdoor experiences, the nearby town of Ranohira is the main base for travelers visiting the park. Here, you'll find a range of accommodation options, from budget guesthouses to mid-range hotels and luxury lodges. Staying in Ranohira allows you to enjoy the conveniences of town while being close to the park entrance.

For those seeking a more immersive experience, several eco-lodges near the park offer a chance to stay within nature's embrace. These lodges are typically built using sustainable practices, ensuring minimal environmental impact while providing comfortable and charming accommodations. Many of these lodges feature stunning views of the surrounding landscape, so you can wake up each morning to the sight of Isalo's majestic canyons.

For a truly unique experience, consider staying in a tented camp or a rustic bungalow near the park. These options allow you to spend the night under the stars, surrounded by the tranquility of Madagascar's wild beauty. However, it's important to book early, especially during peak seasons, as accommodations near the park can fill up quickly.

Guided Tours and Trail Advice

While Isalo National Park is accessible on your own, it is highly recommended to take a guided tour to get the most out of your visit. The park's trails can be challenging, and a knowledgeable guide can ensure you don't miss any of the highlights while providing important insights into the area's flora, fauna, and geological history.

There are several marked trails of varying difficulty, so you can choose a route that fits your physical abilities. Popular trails include the "Canyon des Singes" (Monkey Canyon) and the "Piscine Naturelle" (Natural Pool), both of which offer rewarding views and opportunities to cool off in natural pools. If you're feeling adventurous, the "Namaza Trail" takes you through some of the park's most striking rock formations and offers a glimpse of Madagascar's rich biodiversity.

Your guide will also ensure your safety while navigating the park, as some of the terrain can be rugged, and they can help you identify the best places to spot wildlife. Make sure to ask your guide about the park's history, as Isalo is not only a natural wonder but also a site of cultural significance. It was once considered a sacred place by the Bara people, and there are burial sites within the park that reflect its historical importance.

What to Bring and What to Know

Before heading to Isalo National Park, there are a few essential items you'll need to bring to ensure a comfortable and safe experience. First and foremost, sturdy hiking boots are a must, as the park's trails can be rocky and uneven. A hat and sunglasses will protect you from the sun, as many areas of the park have little shade. Be sure to carry plenty of water, especially if you're hiking for several hours, as the climate can be hot and dry, particularly in the summer months.

Don't forget to pack sunscreen to shield yourself from the intense sun, and insect repellent to protect against mosquitoes, especially when exploring the more tropical areas. A good camera or binoculars will come in handy for capturing the unique wildlife and landscapes you'll encounter along the way.

While the park is generally safe, it's important to be aware of your surroundings and follow your guide's advice. Some of the trails may involve steep climbs, and there can be sudden changes in weather, so it's wise to bring a light jacket for cooler evenings.

Finally, Isalo is a place to respect nature, so remember to stay on the designated trails to help preserve the park's fragile environment. Take your trash with you, and avoid disturbing the wildlife, ensuring that future generations can enjoy this natural wonder just as you have.

Isalo National Park is a place that promises adventure, beauty, and a deep connection to Madagascar's natural heritage. Whether you're hiking through canyons, spotting lemurs, or simply marveling at the stunning landscape, Isalo offers an unforgettable experience for all who visit.

Andasibe-Mantadia – The Lemur Capital

Andasibe-Mantadia is one of the most enchanting places in Madagascar, especially for anyone who dreams of seeing lemurs in their natural habitat. Often called the Lemur Capital, this lush rainforest region is best known for being home to the largest of all lemur species, the Indri. These black and white creatures are known for their haunting, echoing calls that drift through the forest canopy at dawn. Hearing their songs in the stillness of the morning is a moment that stays with you long after you've left the forest.

The Indri lemurs are just one part of what makes Andasibe-Mantadia special. The area is made up of two main parks: the smaller, easily accessible Analamazaotra Reserve and the larger, wilder Mantadia National Park. Both offer exceptional opportunities to explore rich biodiversity, thick rainforest, and well-maintained trails. Walking quietly through these forests often leads to sightings of bamboo lemurs, sifakas, and chameleons hiding in plain sight. The experience is immersive and deeply rewarding.

Early mornings and late afternoons are the best times for nature walks, as this is when wildlife is most active. The forest is alive with sound—the rustle of leaves, the calls of distant animals, and the songs of birds you won't hear anywhere else in the world. Walking with a local guide not only makes it easier to spot elusive creatures but also brings the forest to life with stories and local knowledge.

The best time to visit Andasibe-Mantadia is during the dry season, from April to November. During these months, trails are easier to navigate, and wildlife is more visible. Rain can make paths slippery and some areas difficult to access, so checking weather conditions before you plan your hike is helpful. That said, even in wetter months, the forest has a magical charm—mist rising through the trees, glistening leaves, and fewer visitors make for a quiet, almost mystical experience.

Accommodation around Andasibe ranges from simple lodges to beautifully designed eco-resorts nestled at the edge of the forest. Many of these places are built with the environment in mind and are run in partnership with local communities. Staying in an eco-lodge means you not only get to enjoy comfort and stunning views, but you also support conservation and sustainable tourism. Meals are often made using local ingredients, and dishes reflect the culture and flavors of the area—fresh fruits, rice-based meals, and zebu meat are commonly served, along with Malagasy-style curries and warm, home-cooked stews.

Whether you're waking up to the sound of the forest or ending the day with a quiet dinner under the stars, Andasibe-Mantadia offers a peaceful, unforgettable retreat into Madagascar's wild heart. It's a place where time slows down, and every moment is filled with discovery.

Tsingy de Bemaraha – The Stone Forest

Tsingy de Bemaraha is unlike anything you've ever seen. A vast forest of sharp limestone spires stretching into the sky, this surreal landscape feels more like a scene from a fantasy film than a real place on Earth. Formed over millions of years by water and erosion, the Tsingy—meaning "where one cannot walk barefoot" in the Malagasy language—truly lives up to its name. The towering stone formations, deep gorges, hanging bridges, and hidden caves create a natural maze that is both visually stunning and physically challenging.

Exploring Tsingy de Bemaraha is not for the faint-hearted, but for those with a sense of adventure, the reward is immense. Some parts of the reserve require you to climb, crawl, and balance your way through narrow passages and over suspension bridges that stretch above dramatic drops. Yet every turn brings awe-inspiring views, from jagged stone cathedrals to quiet pockets of forest where lemurs leap through the branches and birds with colorful plumage flash past. It's a place that feels untouched and sacred, a reminder of nature's raw and untamed beauty.

Adventure seekers will find this destination particularly exciting. The park's circuits vary in difficulty, with some easier routes that focus more on scenery and wildlife, and others that require more stamina and climbing skills. Local guides are essential not just for navigating the trails safely, but also for sharing knowledge about the flora and fauna that have adapted to this rocky environment. The park is also home to several species found nowhere else on the planet, making it a paradise for nature lovers and photographers alike.

Reaching Tsingy de Bemaraha requires planning. Located in western Madagascar, the journey involves a combination of road travel and river crossings. Most travelers access the park from the town of Morondava, with a stopover in Belo-sur-Tsiribihina. The route is rough and long, especially during the rainy season, when roads become muddy and sometimes impassable. It's best to make the trip during the dry months, from June to November, when conditions are more reliable and the park is fully open to visitors.

Accommodations near the park are basic but comfortable, often blending with the natural surroundings and offering warm hospitality.

Staying in these lodges gives you a chance to unwind after a day of climbing and exploring. Meals are usually hearty and simple, featuring rice, grilled meats, and local vegetables. Electricity may be limited, but the tradeoff is a deeper connection to nature—stars light up the sky at night, and mornings are filled with the sounds of the wild.

For those willing to go off the beaten path, Tsingy de Bemaraha offers an unforgettable experience. It's not just about the views or the thrill of the hike—it's about stepping into a world that seems to exist beyond time, carved by nature, and protected by its remoteness. Every challenge faced along the way only adds to the sense of wonder when you finally stand among the stone spires and realize you've made it to one of the most extraordinary places on Earth.

CHAPTER 8

HIDDEN GEMS AND OFF-THE-PATH ADVENTURES

Beyond the famous attractions and popular circuits, Madagascar holds countless hidden gems waiting to be discovered. Tucked away from the tourist crowds are serene islands and untouched beaches that offer a more personal, peaceful connection to the island's natural beauty. Places like Île aux Nattes, a small island near Sainte Marie, feel like a secret escape. Its soft white sand, clear turquoise waters, and laid-back atmosphere invite visitors to slow down and soak in the calm. With fewer visitors, the beaches remain pristine and the pace of life unhurried, perfect for travelers seeking rest, reflection, and a deeper appreciation for the quiet rhythms of island living.

Remote coastal villages such as Anakao or Salary Bay bring the same sense of serenity with the added bonus of cultural immersion. Reaching these places might involve long journeys on sandy roads or boat trips over rolling waves, but the rewards include crystal-clear waters, excellent snorkeling, and sunsets that paint the sky in colors that feel unreal. In these out-of-the-way locations, simple pleasures take center stage—fresh seafood meals, hammocks strung between palm trees, and long walks on empty shores.

Inland, Madagascar is also dotted with sacred hills and quiet villages that preserve ancient traditions and deep spiritual ties to the land. The hills of Ambohimanga, for example, are more than scenic—they're places of royal legacy and spiritual importance. Locals believe these hills are protected by ancestral spirits, and they're often used for ceremonies and quiet reflection. Wandering through these areas provides a rare opportunity to connect with the Malagasy people's rich cultural roots. In many of these villages, time seems to move more slowly, and everyday life follows a rhythm passed down through generations. Farmers tend rice paddies, children play along dirt paths, and elders share stories under the shade of old trees.

Exploring these less-visited areas often means stepping outside your comfort zone. Roads can be rough, language barriers may arise, and amenities are limited. But these challenges are part of the adventure. With the help of local guides, travelers not only navigate these places more easily but also gain deeper insight into the traditions, values, and ways of life that define Madagascar beyond its postcards. These off-the-path adventures remind you that the true essence of a place often lies in its quiet corners, in the unpolished beauty of nature, and in the warmth of people who welcome you into their world, even if only for a short while.

Away from the well-known parks and tour circuits, Madagascar is filled with natural reserves that see fewer tourists but offer equally unforgettable encounters with the island's rare wildlife and landscapes. Places like Ankarafantsika National

Park in the northwest or Lokobe Reserve near Nosy Be provide a deeper dive into Madagascar's biodiversity, yet remain relatively quiet compared to the more famous sites. In these lesser-traveled reserves, it's easier to spot elusive animals, enjoy birdwatching without crowds, and feel completely surrounded by untouched nature. The trails might be narrower and the paths more rugged, but the solitude adds to the feeling of true wilderness exploration.

Finding these hidden pockets of nature is only part of the journey—having a trusted local guide makes all the difference. A good guide not only knows the terrain and how to spot wildlife but also shares stories, explains customs, and connects you with the culture that surrounds these natural wonders. Local guides often come from nearby villages and have personal relationships with the environment they work in, which means they approach their role with deep respect and insight. They can point out medicinal plants, call out to rare birds, or mimic lemur sounds to draw them closer.

To find these trusted guides, the best approach is to connect through local tourism offices, eco-lodges, or reputable community-based tour services. Many of these places work directly with certified guides who have received training in both safety and environmental care. Another reliable way is through word-of-mouth recommendations from fellow travelers or platforms that promote ethical travel. Choosing a local guide not only enriches your experience but also supports the community, giving back to the people who protect and care for these extraordinary places.

Taking the road less traveled in Madagascar opens up a side of the island that many never see. The rewards come in the form of quiet discoveries, meaningful connections, and the unforgettable feeling of being part of something both ancient and alive.

CHAPTER 9

THINGS TO DO IN MADAGASCAR

Madagascar is a treasure chest for anyone with a love for nature and adventure. Wildlife watching tops the list, offering a chance to observe animals you won't find anywhere else on Earth. From the curious gaze of lemurs swinging through treetops to the bright colors of chameleons crawling along branches, the island is alive with unique and often surprising creatures. Birdwatchers can enjoy the melodies of endemic species, while night walks in certain parks reveal the nocturnal wonders of this diverse ecosystem. Whether you are deep in the rainforest or exploring open highlands, every step opens a new window into the wild.

For those looking to be more active, Madagascar delivers a wide range of eco-adventures. Hiking is especially rewarding, with trails that lead you through canyons, forests, and along rugged cliffs with breathtaking views. Isalo National Park's rock formations and hidden pools make each hike feel like an unfolding story of ancient earth. In the east, misty paths in Andasibe-Mantadia lead you to the echoing calls of the Indri lemur, while in the Tsingy de Bemaraha, narrow stone paths challenge your balance and sense of wonder.

The coastline invites a different kind of excitement. Snorkeling and diving reveal a world of coral reefs, sea turtles, and vibrant marine life. Nosy Be and its surrounding islets offer crystal-clear waters perfect for both beginners and seasoned swimmers. In the south, Anakao is a peaceful fishing village where you can surf, kiteboard, or simply float in warm lagoons. Whale watching is another seasonal highlight, especially near Île Sainte-Marie, where humpback whales migrate and often leap from the water in dramatic displays.

Whether your idea of fun is tracking rare animals in the forest or gliding across blue waves under the sun, Madagascar lets you create your own adventure story, one filled with discovery, beauty, and unforgettable moments.

Exploring Madagascar isn't just about the landscapes and wildlife. The heart of the island also beats through its people, their traditions, and the way of life in the many villages scattered across the country. Taking part in village tours offers a meaningful opportunity to step into this world. These experiences often begin with a warm welcome, where locals share stories, music, or even a home-cooked meal. Walking through a traditional village reveals how communities live in harmony with nature, grow their own food, and pass down knowledge through generations. Whether it's watching skilled weavers at work or learning how to prepare a local dish, every moment adds depth to your understanding of Madagascar's cultural identity.

Spending time in these places is not about rushing through a list of things to see. It's about slowing down, observing, and connecting. You might be invited to join a local celebration or witness a ritual that reflects the island's blend of beliefs—where ancestral respect meets spiritual practices. These moments often leave the strongest impressions, reminding travelers that Madagascar's beauty is not only seen but felt through genuine human connection.

As the sun sets, the island comes alive in a different way. Night markets pop up in towns and cities, glowing under strings of lights and filled with the aroma of sizzling street food. Stalls display handmade crafts, from embroidered fabrics to wood carvings, each one telling its own story. Walking through these lively spaces, you can sample local snacks, listen to music, and browse souvenirs that support local artisans. Craft shops in smaller towns often double as workshops, where you can see how items are made and even try your hand at a traditional skill.

These cultural experiences make every trip more personal. They go beyond the postcard scenes and bring you into the rhythm of real life in Madagascar—vibrant, welcoming, and full of small surprises that stay with you long after the journey ends.

CHAPTER 10

THINGS YOU SHOULDN'T DO

While Madagascar offers an unforgettable journey filled with natural beauty and rich culture, it's important to understand and respect the local customs and stay aware of certain do's and don'ts to ensure a safe and respectful visit. One of the first things to keep in mind is the concept of "fady," which refers to traditional taboos or sacred customs that vary from region to region. Some fady might prohibit certain behaviors like pointing at sacred places, whistling at night, or touching specific animals or objects. These taboos are deeply respected by the Malagasy people, and breaking them—even unknowingly—can cause offense or discomfort, so it's always helpful to ask a local guide about the local customs wherever you go.

Another common mistake travelers make is dressing too casually in conservative communities.

While beachwear is fine on the coast, it's respectful to dress modestly in villages or during cultural visits. Taking photos of people without asking is also considered impolite, so always seek permission before snapping pictures, especially in sacred or private areas. Loud behavior or openly displaying frustration is generally frowned upon, as Malagasy culture values patience and calmness in social situations. It's also best not to hand out money or sweets to children, as this can encourage unhealthy habits and dependency. Instead, support local businesses, schools, or community projects if you wish to give back.

Apart from social customs, there are a few environmental and safety concerns to keep in mind. Madagascar is home to rare wildlife and delicate ecosystems, so it's essential not to disturb animals, pick plants, or stray from marked trails in protected areas. Littering or leaving plastic waste behind in rural or natural spots contributes to environmental damage and harms local wildlife. Using reef-safe sunscreen and avoiding single-use plastics helps protect Madagascar's unique marine life, especially in coral reef areas.

When it comes to personal safety, avoid walking alone at night in unfamiliar areas, especially in large cities. Keep your valuables secure and be cautious when using ATMs. Stick to bottled or filtered water to prevent stomach issues, and make sure your vaccinations and travel insurance are up to date before arriving. In case of political unrest or severe weather warnings, follow local advice and avoid large gatherings or risky areas.

Respecting local culture and staying mindful of the environment not only helps you stay safe but also shows appreciation for the island and its people. Traveling with awareness and humility enriches your experience and helps ensure Madagascar remains a welcoming place for all who visit.

When exploring a country as culturally rich and diverse as Madagascar, being mindful of your words, appearance, and behavior can go a long way in creating respectful and meaningful connections with the locals. Some phrases or topics are best avoided in conversation, especially when speaking about politics, poverty, or making comparisons between cultures in a way that may come off as judgmental. Sarcasm or humor that relies on cultural stereotypes can easily be misunderstood, so it's best to keep your tone friendly and sincere. Being overly critical of local services or infrastructure, even if unintentional, may seem disrespectful. Instead, showing curiosity and gratitude helps foster good will and understanding.

In terms of clothing, it's important to strike a balance between comfort and modesty. Revealing clothes might be acceptable on the beach, but when walking through towns or visiting villages and sacred places, it's best to wear garments that cover your shoulders and knees. This is especially important for women, as modest dress is often seen as a sign of respect. For men, avoiding overly casual clothing like sleeveless shirts in formal or traditional settings is equally important. It's also wise to avoid wearing camouflage clothing, which can sometimes be associated with military personnel and may cause confusion or unwanted attention.

When it comes to photography, always ask before taking pictures of people, especially in rural areas. Some communities may view photography as intrusive or even disrespectful if done without permission. Avoid photographing military facilities, police officers, and airports, as this may be prohibited or raise suspicion. Sacred sites, tombs, and ceremonies should also be approached with sensitivity, and if in doubt, it's better to politely ask or refrain altogether.

Maintaining good health during your trip starts with hygiene awareness and smart daily habits. Always carry hand sanitizer or antibacterial wipes, especially when traveling to remote areas with limited facilities. Stick to bottled or filtered water, even for brushing your teeth, and avoid ice unless you're sure it's made from purified water. Be cautious with street food, and choose vendors with good hygiene practices and a steady flow of customers. Fruits that you peel yourself, like bananas or oranges, are generally safe, but raw salads or undercooked meats can carry bacteria that upset your stomach.

It's also important to wash your hands frequently and avoid touching your face, especially after handling money or traveling on public transport. Insect repellent is a must in areas where mosquitoes are present, particularly to prevent bites that may spread malaria or dengue. Lastly, if you're feeling unwell, don't delay seeking help. Local pharmacies can offer assistance, and in more serious cases, private clinics in larger cities are usually well equipped to provide care. A little preparation and cautious behavior will help ensure your trip to Madagascar is not only enriching, but also smooth and enjoyable from start to finish.

CHAPTER 11

SAMPLE ITINERARIES

If you only have three days to experience Madagascar, focusing on culture and convenience is the best way to make the most of your short stay. Begin your journey in Antananarivo, the country's capital and cultural heart. Spend your first day exploring the historic Old Upper Town, where narrow cobbled streets lead you past colonial buildings, royal landmarks, and local markets full of color and charm. Visit the Queen's Palace for sweeping views and insights into the island's royal past, then relax at a nearby café with Malagasy coffee and street snacks.

On the second day, take a short trip east to Ambohimanga, a UNESCO World Heritage site and spiritual landmark. The drive is not long, and the peaceful atmosphere of the royal hilltop village offers a window into the traditions of Madagascar's highlands. Afterward, head back to the capital to visit handicraft markets, try some local dishes like romazava or vary amin'anana, and enjoy live music at a laid-back venue in the city.

For your final day, consider a visit to Lemurs' Park, located just outside Antananarivo. It's a great chance to see various species of lemurs up close in a semi-natural environment. This visit provides a gentle but memorable wildlife experience before you return to the city for some last-minute shopping or a stroll around Lake Anosy. Although brief, this three-day trip gives you a snapshot of Madagascar's unique blend of history, culture, and nature.

If you have a full week to explore, a seven-day adventure opens up more of Madagascar's breathtaking natural wonders. Start in Antananarivo for one night to get oriented and rest from your travels. The next morning, head east to Andasibe-Mantadia National Park, which is about a three-hour drive. Spend two days in the lush rainforest exploring the trails, listening to the calls of the indri lemurs, and enjoying a stay at an eco-lodge surrounded by nature.

From Andasibe, continue south toward Antsirabe, a charming town known for its colonial charm, thermal springs, and rickshaws. Spend a night here, soaking in the relaxed atmosphere and enjoying a traditional Malagasy meal. Then drive on to Ranomafana National Park, one of Madagascar's top wildlife destinations. With misty forests, hot springs, and rare species, two days here offers both adventure and serenity. Hire a local guide for the best experience and don't forget your camera.

Wrap up your itinerary by returning to Antananarivo, either directly or with a stopover in Ambositra, famous for its wood carving and art. Once back in the capital, enjoy a farewell dinner, perhaps with a view over the city, reflecting on your week of discovery. This one-week plan offers a well-balanced taste of Madagascar's wild beauty, warm culture, and quiet charm.

If you have two full weeks to explore Madagascar, you're in for an unforgettable journey that allows for a deeper dive into the island's stunning diversity. With the extra time, you can experience everything from lush rainforests and rocky deserts to paradise beaches and vibrant cities. A well-planned 14-day trip lets you mix adventure with relaxation, cultural immersion with wildlife watching, and remote escapes with comfortable stays.

Begin your exploration in Antananarivo, where you'll settle in and explore the capital's historic landmarks and buzzing local markets. After a night in the city, head east to Andasibe-Mantadia National Park. Spend two days soaking in the forest trails, watching indri lemurs leap from tree to tree, and enjoying the serenity of an eco-lodge tucked in nature. From there, return to the capital briefly before flying to the northwestern coast and landing in Nosy Be.

Spend the next few days unwinding on Nosy Be's beaches, snorkeling in the clear waters of Nosy Tanikely, or joining a boat tour around nearby islands. With vibrant nightlife, fresh seafood, and laid-back charm, it's a great mid-trip break before heading inland again. From Nosy Be, travel south toward Morondava for a stop at the iconic Avenue of the Baobabs. Time your visit for sunset and you'll witness the trees glowing in golden light, creating a dreamlike memory.

Next, journey to the southwest to explore the otherworldly Tsingy de Bemaraha. The limestone pinnacles and rope bridges offer thrilling walks and jaw-dropping views. After a few days of adventure, head southeast to Isalo National Park for dramatic canyons, desert landscapes, and hidden waterfalls. Here, hikes are scenic and manageable, with chances to spot ring-tailed lemurs and swim in natural pools.

Afterward, continue to the coastal town of Ifaty or Anakao for some final days of beach relaxation and snorkeling in warm, turquoise waters. The local fishing villages and coral reefs are quiet and less commercial, giving you space to reflect on the journey. End your trip by making your way back to Antananarivo, either by domestic flight or overland route, depending on your pace and preference.

For travelers with specific interests, the route can be customized:

For Beach Lovers: Focus your route on Nosy Be, Nosy Iranja, Ifaty, and Anakao. Spread your time across coastal lodges, island hopping, and diving excursions, with a brief inland stop at Isalo for a desert-meets-oasis experience.

For Wildlife Enthusiasts: Prioritize Andasibe, Ranomafana, Ankarafantsika, and Tsingy de Bemaraha. These parks offer chances to see Madagascar's rarest animals, from leaf-tailed geckos to dancing sifakas, all in their natural habitats.

For Culture Seekers: Include Antananarivo, Ambositra, Antsirabe, and smaller villages like Ambohimanga and Ifanadiana. Visit artisan markets, sacred sites, and local homes to learn about Malagasy crafts, beliefs, and traditions.

No matter your route, a 14-day journey gives you time to fall in love with Madagascar's layered beauty, and leaves you with lasting stories to tell.

CHAPTER 12

RESPONSIBLE TRAVEL IN MADAGASCAR

When traveling in Madagascar, it's important to approach your adventure with mindfulness and respect, ensuring that your visit contributes to the preservation of the island's unique environment and supports its local communities. The nation's biodiversity and rich cultural heritage are its most valuable assets, and how you interact with both can have a long-lasting impact.

Respecting Nature and Wildlife

Madagascar is home to some of the most unique ecosystems and species on the planet, including lemurs, chameleons, and an array of plants that can't be found anywhere else. To protect these irreplaceable treasures, always follow local guidelines and regulations in national parks and reserves. Keep a safe distance from wildlife, refrain from feeding animals, and avoid disrupting their natural behaviors. When hiking, stay on designated paths to minimize your impact on fragile ecosystems. If you're fortunate enough to see rare species, remember that your presence should be a privilege, not an entitlement.

Another important way to protect nature is by reducing your environmental footprint. Use reusable water bottles, avoid plastic packaging, and be conscious of waste disposal. Many parts of Madagascar struggle with waste management, so make sure you dispose of trash responsibly, and always pick up after yourself. Whenever possible, choose eco-friendly accommodations, lodges, and tour operators who prioritize sustainability and conservation. These businesses typically operate in ways that minimize environmental damage while promoting responsible tourism practices.

Supporting Local Businesses and Communities

One of the most impactful ways to travel responsibly in Madagascar is by supporting local businesses and communities. Madagascar's economy heavily relies on tourism, so your choices can make a significant difference to local livelihoods. Opt for locally owned accommodations, guides, and restaurants to ensure that the money spent on your trip stays within the community. Local guides, in particular, provide an authentic experience and offer valuable insights into the culture and environment that you won't find in guidebooks. Many of these guides are trained in sustainable tourism and conservation efforts, making them an essential part of responsible travel.

In addition to supporting tourism-related businesses, consider purchasing locally made crafts, textiles, and artworks as souvenirs. By doing so, you're not only acquiring a meaningful keepsake, but you're also directly benefiting artisans and their families. Look for fair-trade organizations or markets that guarantee that the artists are compensated fairly for their work.

When engaging with communities, always approach with respect and an open mind. Malagasy culture is diverse and vibrant, and there's a lot to learn from the people you meet. If you're invited into someone's home or community, be gracious and follow their lead in terms of customs and behavior. This also extends to photography: always ask permission before taking someone's photo, especially in rural areas where people may prefer their privacy.

As you explore Madagascar, consider that your presence can help fund conservation efforts and support sustainable development. Many national parks and reserves rely on entry fees and donations to maintain their work. Whether it's a ticket to a park or a contribution to a local environmental initiative, your investment in these programs can help ensure that future generations can experience Madagascar's wonders as you did.

By traveling responsibly, you'll not only have a richer, more fulfilling experience but also leave a positive legacy for the people and places you visit.

Reducing Waste and Traveling Sustainably

Traveling sustainably goes beyond simply visiting a destination. It's about making choices that reduce your environmental impact and help preserve the places you love to explore. In Madagascar, this is especially important given the island's fragile ecosystems and its efforts to balance tourism with conservation.

One of the most effective ways to reduce waste during your trip is by minimizing plastic consumption. Madagascar, like many places, is still working on effective waste management systems, and plastic pollution is a significant concern. Carry a reusable water bottle and fill it up at your accommodation or local refill stations. Avoid single-use plastic bags, straws, and bottles by bringing your own shopping bag, and say no to items packaged in plastic whenever possible. Many local markets are willing to wrap your purchases in banana leaves or reusable cloth bags, which are environmentally friendly alternatives.

When it comes to food packaging, try to choose restaurants and food vendors that prioritize local, fresh ingredients and sustainable practices. Avoid takeaway food that comes with excess packaging, and bring your own container when possible. Similarly, when staying at hotels or eco-lodges, check if they recycle or have waste separation systems in place, and make sure you're adhering to their policies.

Another key area is water conservation. In Madagascar, water can be scarce in some regions, so be mindful of your usage. Simple habits like taking shorter showers, turning off the tap while brushing your teeth, and using water-saving devices in accommodations can all contribute to responsible water usage.

Opt for sustainable transport options where possible. For example, when traveling around the island, consider using shared transportation methods, like buses or minibuses, instead of taxis or private cars, as this reduces the number of vehicles on the road. Additionally, walking or biking when exploring cities or towns is not only eco-friendly but also a great way to experience the local culture up close.

Lastly, many eco-friendly tour operators in Madagascar focus on minimizing the carbon footprint of their activities. Look for tours that use electric vehicles, bicycles, or offer walking and hiking tours, which allow you to experience nature without harming it.

What It Means to Be a Mindful Visitor

Being a mindful visitor means adopting a conscious approach to your travels that is rooted in respect, understanding, and care for the destination you're visiting. It's not just about the environment, but also about the people and cultures you encounter. In Madagascar, the customs and traditions vary widely from region to region, and approaching each with an open heart and a willingness to learn will enrich your experience.

A mindful visitor takes time to understand and appreciate the local culture. This might involve learning a few words in Malagasy or French, greeting locals in a respectful manner, and asking about customs before engaging in activities. By doing so, you show that you're not just a tourist passing through, but a traveler who is genuinely interested in the culture and heritage of the country.

In addition, a mindful traveler takes into consideration the social impact of their actions. Be aware of the challenges faced by local communities and be conscious of your presence in rural or remote areas. For instance, while it may be tempting to buy crafts or souvenirs from children or street vendors, consider the larger picture. Some forms of child labor or exploitation may be a reality in certain areas, and it's important to support businesses and initiatives that promote fair wages and ethical practices.

Being mindful also means practicing patience. Madagascar's pace of life is different from what you might be accustomed to, so don't rush through your trip. Take time to savor each moment, whether it's sitting in a local café, enjoying a wildlife tour, or simply walking through a village. Embrace the slower rhythm, as it's part of the island's charm.

Another essential aspect of being a mindful visitor is considering your carbon footprint. While Madagascar is an island, many travelers arrive by plane, contributing to the island's carbon emissions. Though there are no direct alternatives to flying, there are ways to offset your travel impact. Some airlines and travel agencies offer carbon offset programs that allow you to contribute to environmental projects, like reforestation or renewable energy initiatives, to balance out the emissions from your flight.

Lastly, a mindful traveler practices responsible behavior when it comes to wildlife. Madagascar is renowned for its incredible biodiversity, but it's crucial to respect animals in their natural habitats. Avoid disturbing wildlife, refrain from feeding animals, and choose eco-tours that emphasize conservation and education rather than exploitation.

In essence, being a mindful visitor means being aware of the impact of your travel on both the environment and the local people, making choices that enhance rather than diminish the places you visit, and embracing a deeper connection with the world around you. When you travel with mindfulness, you help create a more sustainable future for all.

CONCLUSION

Final Travel Tips and Encouragement

As you prepare for your journey to Madagascar, keep in mind that this adventure is not just about visiting a new destination, but about embracing a unique experience—one that connects you to nature, culture, and the people of this magical island. Madagascar is a place that invites you to slow down, explore its wonders with curiosity, and immerse yourself in its beauty, all while respecting its delicate environment and vibrant communities.

Before you set off, remember to plan ahead. Ensure you have your travel documents in order, take care of any health precautions, and pack wisely for the diverse experiences ahead. Whether you're traveling for wildlife encounters, cultural immersion, or outdoor adventures, preparation is key. But also, be flexible. Things may not always go according to plan, but that's part of the charm of exploring a destination as unique as Madagascar.

Stay open to the surprises, learn from the unexpected, and embrace the moments that make travel truly memorable.

Most importantly, take time to be present. While the landscapes and wildlife are awe-inspiring, it's the people and experiences that will leave a lasting impression. Engage with the locals, respect their traditions, and contribute positively to the communities you visit. Your adventure isn't just about the places you'll see but about how you experience them and the connections you make along the way.

Reflecting on the Journey Before It Begins

Madagascar offers more than just a destination—it's an invitation to step into a world unlike any other. The island's biodiversity, rich culture, and stunning landscapes will captivate your senses and challenge your perceptions. From the towering baobabs to the playful lemurs, from the pristine beaches to the remote hills, each corner of Madagascar holds a story waiting to be discovered.

As you reflect on this journey before you embark, think about what draws you to this remarkable island. Is it the chance to witness nature's raw beauty? To immerse yourself in a culture that is both ancient and evolving? Or perhaps it's the desire to disconnect from the hustle and bustle of everyday life and reconnect with nature? Whatever your reason, know that Madagascar promises a transformative experience, one that will stay with you long after you've left its shores.

Your Madagascar Adventure Awaits

So, pack your bags, grab your camera, and get ready for an adventure that will awaken your sense of wonder. Madagascar's vibrant landscapes, wildlife, and people are ready to share their magic with you. This is your chance to be part of something truly special—an adventure that will change the way you see the world and leave you with memories that will last a lifetime.

Your Madagascar adventure awaits, and it's ready to be discovered. Take the leap, and let this incredible island surprise you at every turn.

Made in the USA
Middletown, DE
01 May 2025